MASTERS AT WORK

MASTERS AT WORK

BECOMING A LIFE COACH

TOM CHIARELLA

SIMON & SCHUSTER

New York   London   Toronto   Sydney   New Delhi

Simon & Schuster
1230 Avenue of the Americas
New York, NY 10020

Copyright © 2019 by Simon & Schuster, Inc.

First Simon & Schuster hardcover edition September 2019

SIMON & SCHUSTER and colophon are registered trademarks of
Simon & Schuster, Inc.

For information about special discounts for bulk purchases, please contact Simon
& Schuster Special Sales at 1-866-506-1949 or business@simonandschuster.com.

The Simon & Schuster Speakers Bureau can bring authors to your live event. For
more information or to book an event, contact the Simon & Schuster Speakers
Bureau at 1-866-248-3049 or visit our website at www.simonspeakers.com.

Manufactured in the United States of America

1   3   5   7   9   10   8   6   4   2

Library of Congress Cataloging-in-Publication Data

ISBN 978-1-5011-9768-0
ISBN 978-1-5011-9770-3 (ebook)

CONTENTS

BECOMING A
LIFE COACH

———————

INTRODUCTION

Children learn early on who to trust and who to ask for help. Some of these individuals come attached to their lives—mothers and fathers, the favorite aunt from Virginia. Others are the result of happenstance—the second-grade teacher who limped a little, the youth minister who loved spy novels, the grumpy neighbor who knew how to grill and sail. Or maybe just that one kid who made everything look easy in school. If all goes well, life presents children with choices when it comes to asking for help.

As an adult, it's harder to know who to trust. We all have friends, but friends can be fools. Unwise. Still learning. Not every friend has the wisdom or experience to grapple with the nuances of careers, the ups and downs of relationships, the challenges of parenting. These are issues that friends might be beginning to face themselves, and so they are just as likely to ask you for help as you are to ask them. In the workplace, it can be worse. Not every job presents a colleague who can be trusted for good advice. And not every friend or coworker can be counted on to tell you the truth even if it hurts your feelings. And sometimes you just need the truth. Sigh. Brutal, brutal sigh.

We are creatures of connection. We want friends. And yes, we need help from time to time. We seek out teachers. Mentors. Spiritual guides. Someone who helped make the right choice when we were hurting. A coworker who modeled the right way to go to work, the right attitude, the right energy, the right set of expectations.

We turn to others. We ask for help. Wise people, leaders, friends, kind souls, experienced people, people who have suffered and triumphed, teachers, coaches. Once, they were all around us, it seems. But somehow it becomes difficult to find them when we get older.

Enter the life coach.

LIFE COACHES ARE INDIVIDUALS who make themselves available for consultation and guidance. They are expert in helping others create positive change in their lives or careers. Typically, they concentrate on such issues as work-life balance, personal health, time management, and stress reduction. But effective coaching extends into an examination of daily habits, the way we treat others, the way we think about our work, and the way we speak about ourselves and judge our own actions.

Maybe that seems like a wordy way to define friendship. While a life coach may be kind, caring, and, yes, friendly, a life coach is not a friend. They are professionals who act as your advocate and behavioral analyst. For money. They don't provide answers. They work to help you find the answers yourself. They help you get the best from you. As such, they aren't likely to talk about themselves. Ever. They are trained not to. There's nothing newsy, or gossipy, about conversations with a life coach. When you hire one, you are the client. Not the pal. They will ask the client to speak about themselves, they'll expect honesty, and they'll work to hold the client accountable for their behavior.

Some picture the relationship with a life coach as a series of lunches where you get advice from a senior colleague or old friend. Rule one with good life coaches? Life coaches don't give advice. They help clients get a fresh look at their own process of decision making. They deconstruct motivation. They disassemble habits into their constituent parts. Life coaching attempts to present the client with questions that allow them to connect to a future offering new possibilities. The life coach doesn't promise to know how the client will get anywhere. They help the client see that they have the tools to make choices without the crutch of someone else's advice.

Any life coach will tell you: they're not a friend. They may add: Not a mentor. Not a therapist. Not a spiritual guide. Not a teacher. But they *do* operate in the territories of these human relationships. When their clients talk about them, they use the very terms we use when discussing friends, mentors, therapists, spiritual guides, and teachers. There are examples of gratitude, devotion, appreciation, allegiance, and even love from clients in the comments you find on the web pages of most life coaches. They make people think, they give some advice, and they get paid for that. How hard can it be?

WHAT DOES IT TAKE to become a life coach? You don't need a license. There isn't any such thing. And life coaching isn't particularly regulated on the federal or state level. There is no authoritative private or public oversight of the field. No standard certification process. And while there are certification programs, there is no agreed-upon curriculum from one program to the next, and neither is there any standard coaching technique that bridges the gaps between the various programs.

In many ways, becoming a life coach is simply a matter of declaring: "I'm a life coach." That's really all it takes. So you could be forgiven for having considered life coaching an elaborate scam, and those who practice the job to be flimflam men. But you'll find throughout the pages of this book that quite the opposite is the case. While it may be an amorphous field populated at the fringes by a menagerie of free agents, it is an emergent profession that truly helps a hungry clientele. Its practitioners are genuine and impassioned professionals.

How do they do it? What are their techniques? Some life coaches pose a single revealing question at the start, or conclusion, of each session. They might ask the client to reflect or write a response before the next meeting. That response might be a list. A story. An essay. It might sound more like a mission statement. It may be a description of a street the client lived on. There is no standard exercise. Assignments depend on the instinct and training of the individual life coach.

Other coaches employ Neuro Linguistic Programming to interrupt lifelong patterns of self-image revealed in the way a client describes themself, for instance. The coach assesses: Does the client describe themself by looking at the past? Do they reference mistakes they've typically made? Are they able to describe their plans in terms of the effect of the success they hope to experience? The life coach might then reveal a possible change in habits as small as simple diction. The Neuro Linguistic Programming (NLP)–trained coach may measure a client's eye movements while talking, and ask them to use tapping techniques and pressure points on the body's meridians to interrupt previous patterns of cognition. It is a complex and much-vetted process of guiding a client toward language and self-assessment as a tool of positive change.

Meanwhile, in another wing of the coaching field, executive coaches often ask business clients to use the very tools of business—punch lists, PowerPoint presentations, and action plans—to assess personal habits such as emotional response to others, attention to loved ones, and self-care. These coaches use these tools of business to better connect their clients' potential of the personal self to the best practices of the business self.

We'll better understand it when we get into the heads of the coaches in this book, but it should be clear these are not the only techniques available. Every good coach brings their own tools, and an eclectic array of instinct and experience, to the job. Life coaches are as individual as the fingerprint created by their professional careers and their personal passions.

As RECENTLY AS 1980, there were no declared life coaches, not anywhere really. The term itself did not exist. Now life coaching is a one-billion-dollar industry in this country, two billion worldwide. The International Coach Federation (one of those aforementioned life-coach-accreditation organizations) puts the number of active full-time life coaches at 53,000 worldwide. One-third of them are working in the United States, where they are reported to make between $27,100 and $73,100 a year. Most life coaches freelance, using their books, and speaking and social media platforms, to create and inspire a client base, with whom they communicate through meetings over the phone, on the internet, and face-to-face. Another segment of coaches is retained by employers to work with staff in-house—through mentorship programs, presentations, and in one-on-one sessions. Once, coaching was a service restricted to top-end executives, but now fewer than 5 percent of coaches are assigned solely to senior executives, and many companies (such as internet retail giant Zappos) offer coaching from an in-house staff to all employees. The ICF notes that specialty coaches often make considerably more money than other kinds of coaches. It's clear that life coaching can provide a steady, lucrative side gig or a rewarding full-time career.

The life-coaching career path emerged in the past forty years from a mishmash of decades-old sources and initiatives. Some tie its roots to Werner Erhard's est movement. Others to the rise of self-help learning in the late seventies. But the creation of life coaching may in many ways be credited to the work of American financial planner Thomas Leonard, who held his first coaching sessions out of his office and home in the early eighties. In 1992, he founded Coach University, a virtual coach training school. He further solidified his legacy as a leader in coach training when he published *The Portable Coach* in 2000.

Leonard's work in *The Portable Coach* further developed the curriculum of life-coaching certification programs everywhere. The foundation of the book is a list: twenty-eight principles to create a more successful and inspiring personal and professional life. The list is composed of a set of general principles for living that coaches are urged to live by and guide their clients to live by (like most life coaches who followed in his wake, Leonard believed prospective life coaches should engage their own life coaches in preparation for their careers). Generally speaking, they are wise words, which require a measure of reflection before they sink in. Almost two decades after the book's publication, these principles offer a surprisingly contemporary to-do list of human behaviors. The list includes statements like:

Become incredibly selfish. Put yourself first. Be more independent and less "pulled" by your roles. Always remember that if it's good for you, it's probably good for others. Clearly communicate to others what you want and who you are. This way, people can relax and will expect less of you, thus reducing possible interpersonal conflicts.

Say no when you can just as easily say yes; build that muscle if it's weak.

Sensitize yourself. Identify and reduce numbing behaviors, environments, situations, or emotional blocks. Identify and eliminate the source of adrenaline rushes in your life. Stop stressing yourself.

Unhook yourself from the future; focus on the "now." Free yourself of the worries of tomorrow and yesterday. Always affirm yourself: "I'll focus completely on my family while I'm with them and totally on work while I'm at work." A smooth and secure present-time orientation is the most effective way to attract a better future. Give up a lifelong dream that hasn't been progressing well.

Put all of your goals aside for thirty days and just do what you feel like doing each day.

Identify three "if . . . then" formulae in your life, meaning things you are doing now in order to have something later, and instead, work on the "then" (the ultimate goal) directly.

THIS PROCESS OF REFLECTION, followed by behavior transformation, becomes the laboratory of coach and client, and the principles behind the process are a kind of persistent reference point for both coach and client.

By the mid-nineties Leonard was involved in the initial

efforts to standardize the training of life coaches, founding Coach University, or Coach U, which offered sessions via teleconferencing. This involved students from around the country telephoning in to participate in classes composed of a single thirty-way phone call among students, teachers, and mentors. Leonard died in 2003, at forty-seven, before the emergence of online courses. He did, though, get to see and participate in the expansion of the legitimized life-coaching field.

Since then, life coaches have slipped into every level of our culture. At the top sits a figure like Tony Robbins, who might be considered part life coach, part self-improvement guru, entrepreneur, financial adviser, and self-help author. Starting as a pitchman for another motivational speaker at seventeen years old, Robbins became an early practitioner of Neuro Linguistic Programming. Over the course of four decades, he developed his life-coach work through the gamut of sales platforms—DVD sales, infomercials, webinars, print and digital publishing, social media, high-end retreats, and streaming video. His personal fortune is estimated at $480 million. But with all due respect, Tony Robbins is irrelevant here.

Here we examine the habits and patterns, the professional rules of men and women who are currently earning their way in the field, by refining what they practice while staying in remunerated, one-on-one communication with clients. The coaches profiled here are accessible, hungry for work, and eager to find new clientele to improve their own prospects. They walk the path of their own self-development while working to service their clients' survival and success. Sure, their career field may not have existed thirty years ago, but life coaches have been among us in some form all along. What makes one better than another? How do they grade their own success? How does the client grade their worth? What does the field offer you in terms of opportunity? What kind of person becomes a life coach? Why? And how? What is it really like to be one?

The opportunity to establish a coaching specialization in a growing market of niche services makes the matter of certification more difficult. A quick survey of the internet reveals a collection of specialties that range from the generic and corporate to the very specific and somewhat eccentric.

Fifteen minutes on the internet produced the following list of kinds of coaching available:

- Corporate coaching
- Executive coaching

- Spiritual coaching
- Second-career coaching
- Communication coaching
- Business coaching
- Brand coaching
- Dating coaching
- Intimacy coaching
- Sex coaching
- Foreplay coaching
- Career coaching
- Relationship coaching
- Performance coaching
- Financial coaching
- Retirement coaching
- Addiction coaching
- Porn addiction coaching
- Time management coaching
- Nutrition coaching
- Weight and body image coaching
- Work/life balance coaching
- Carbon coaching (helping others reduce their carbon footprint)

Determining a niche is a key way for a new life coach to establish themselves in the competitive world of client building and social media. It's hard to imagine that Thomas Leonard could have pictured a field called "brand coaching" twenty years ago, although it is a thriving subsection of the field now. These coaching specialties are equally unregulated, and the list of specialties grows.

DESPITE THE FACT THAT so many people, whether certified by programs like Coach U or not, are making so much money by dipping their fingers into life coaching, maybe *because* of that fact, people still question the legitimacy of life coaching. One of the coaches profiled in this book, Gregory Diehl, describes the field as straddling a nebulous "middle zone between the work of a psychologist and a really good friend." Diehl is a life coach who promises to "strategically antagonize" his clients. He breaks down a client's core values so they can be more accurately self-examined. So, not a psychologist, since a psychologist diagnoses and treats individuals suffering from psychological distress. Diehl believes that his clients have the tools to redefine their lives and individual limitations . . . He's more a cryptic sensei.

Not quite your typical "really good friend" either, Diehl is more like a demanding philosophy professor. Yet he has a loyal client list, and a successful publishing business based on his practice that has allowed him to live in fifty countries in the last twelve years while developing a rabid following that craves his brand of confrontational counsel.

So: therapist-teacher, teacher-friend, friend-mentor. Which is it?

It is all of them, of course, and not quite any one in particular.

These sorts of paradigms are often relied on in the understanding of the sometimes nebulous position of life coaching in the culture. The apparent contradictions are normal. The International Coach Federation uses a consultant-therapist-mentor blend. Another coach profiled in this book, Markita Collins, an ordained minister and motivational speaker, toes the line between pastor and entrepreneurial advocate. Executive coach Farrell Reynolds of Woodstock, New York, an early graduate of the Coach U program, asserts to all his incoming clients that he is neither "therapist nor squash buddy." With him, it's not all touchy-feely. He proceeds to vex his clients by centering his teaching on a set of four rules of business of his own making. He's one part Jungian soothsayer, one part corporate sales consultant.

Thomas Leonard himself suggested that it is the responsibility of every life coach to be able to cogently define what a life coach does for a client. It's not what people think it is. The understanding may be greater now, with coaches specializing in life moments from the professional to the personal. They are successful because, as active entrepreneurs themselves, they have found ways to target specific client bases. On some level they are promoters. Developers. Hustlers. As if they'd modeled themselves after Leonard's list, they are insanely selfish, confident in their abilities, and capable of marketing themselves to an audience eager to benefit from their expertise.

In this book you'll also meet Pervis Taylor, a former employee of Def Jam Recordings and the Grammys, who racked up a small collection of film and television credits during his time as an actor and model. In the years since, he's earned an MS in clinical psychology from Columbia University. He is a licensed minister, motivational speaker, and author. Like many other coaches, he has no office. No storefront. No stand-alone professional address. He works from his laptop, and from his phone, and relishes the freedom that comes with taking his job with him wherever he goes.

Amy Moser, a fifty-year-old American living in London, has turned her in-house corporate life-coach training into passionate work in the mentorship of school-age kids. Moser works with a London-based educational organization called Children First, which uses life-coaching techniques to mentor students through bullying, trauma, and social anxiety.

In this book, we are looking at working life coaches. They are writers, speakers, ministers, former executives, parents, travelers, entrepreneurs, social media experts, teachers, and publishers. Some offer therapeutic comfort and the prospect of development. Some appear to offer a kind of friendship. Others are cranky, at times purposely belligerent. There is no single path that a life coach follows. It is a wide and varied field of individual professionals, all going about it in their own way. Here, then, five life coaches, three of whom graduated from accredited life-coaching institutions and two of whom assembled their own credentials. This book doesn't take a position in the debate over certification. No one in these pages is much interested in arguing the superiority of one path over another. They all make a living at it. We don't have a horse in that race. Period.

The life coaches you will meet are engaged in the practice of the job: assembling paying clients, and then helping those clients acquire insight, rather than handing out a list of actionable behaviors to help them dig out from whatever impasse they're facing. They are life coaches. Paid to pay attention to the interests and behaviors of one client at a time.

These coaches share a set of constants. They *don't* give out advice. They *don't* provide answers. They continually revisit their own practices, updating and maintaining their codes of professional behavior. In today's world, they must work to make their voices broadly heard through social media, and work to become brands of their own, appealing and influential to a potential client base. And for their clients, the life coach must operate as a private linchpin of personal choice and professional development.

WE WILL LOOK AT the specific clients of our life coaches to get a feeling for what life coaching has offered them. We'll examine how sessions unfold, and what progress actually looks like. Surprisingly, we'll find occasional skepticism about their profession from the life coaches themselves. We'll encounter the real devotion their clients feel toward them.

You'll see that the real work of personal change is the responsibility of the client. A successful life coach leads others to a place where change is a matter of their own conscious choices.

The life coaches themselves will work to define what it is they do. That's their responsibility. But they will often tell you just as clearly how the stakes are different, and what they are not. It will feel arguable, if not a bit dodgy. Like any human, life coaches can be puzzles. Their work demands some reflection. Somewhere along the way, you may discover if you have the talent and the understanding to become one yourself.

1

NOT A THERAPIST

Pervis Taylor, 33
Brooklyn, NY

It's 9:00 a.m. and along the streets of Brooklyn, Pervis Taylor carries his work in his front pocket. He's a life coach after all. His cell phone is his best tool. The majority of his sessions take place on it, or on his laptop. He's a bright young guy, thirty-eight years old, African American, with a loosely-cropped haircut, featuring a patch of bright white hair on the right side of his head.

Pervis, born in Texas, lives in Brooklyn and has been a life coach for six years. According to his website, he specializes in work with "young professionals and youth of all ages." He deals with issues of masculinity and trauma, and has lately been creating a program to give young men of color a way to speak out about pain in their lives. A writer (he has three books available on his website), he's gentle in his demeanor but tough in his examination of his clients' problems.

Why start with Pervis Taylor? Well, he's young. So you might question his wisdom and experience. But at the same time, he's firmly established in his career, having made his living entirely from coaching for years now. Book royalties, presentations, appearance fees, one-on-one coaching sessions—all these have lent his career a look and a feeling of legitimacy. He has made as much as $90,000 in a given year and as little as $35,000 (slightly less when he was starting out). He connects to young people easily and readily. He has clients in the movie business. He has celebrity clients. He has written books, developed videos of his work. He is broadly qualified, with a master's degree in clinical psychology from Columbia University, yet he has veered away from the practice of psychology because he finds life coaching more liberating.

He is unafraid of stating his feelings about religion, frequently citing his background as a Christian minister, but he actively counsels many clients who claim no religious affiliation. In those cases, he does not seek converts. His job won't allow that. As a life coach, he says, his role is to draw the best decisions from the clients.

It's no surprise when he answers my call from the streets

of the city. It's morning, and the background is a ruckus. Cacophonous. For a moment, it sounds like a piece of heavy machinery is toppling from a rooftop onto the pavement.

He's promised to outline a day in his life as life coach, and starts in fast: "On Mondays, typically I wake up and pray, and then I go into the gym. I'm out of the gym by nine thirty. I send out some social media with my #BEGREAT hashtag. I never miss a day."

He updates Instagram, Twitter, and Facebook every morning. He has people who count on him there. And he's proud of his carefully constructed messages. He takes time every day to reflect on upcoming sessions with clients, for which he keeps a log and notes toward questions he might ask. He's been constructing a daylong presentation with another life coach, which he's hoping to implement as a long-term, extracurricular component with some outer-borough high schools. Then there is the outreach to potential clients. "It's like any job. I'm not doing it well if I'm not dealing with every facet of the work," he says. "Life coaching is much more than phoning a friend. I like giving my clients the time they need, but I need to be prepared for every call. I want to give them work to do, pose questions for them. Give them thoughts to rely on."

Social media has certain principles of success, behaviors that lead to an expanding clientele. Including the frequency and timeliness of posting. Every day Pervis crafts an inspirational thought, hashtags it with his proprietary phrase (#BEGREAT!), and posts as close as possible to the same time as the day before.

His Facebook page is cross-promotional, one part life coach, one part youth minister. His Instagrams are casually illustrative, but accurate—where he is, who he's with, and what excites him today. In his group meetings, he uses video to give voice to the young men of color he's meeting in his early group presentations. He sometimes transports these moments to the social media channels as inspiration to newbie client, casual viewer, and avid follower alike. Every expression on social media is a representation of his trust in the process. He further documents his various appearances, on radio and speaking engagements. He ends many of his entries with his simple assertion #BEGREAT, often enough so that it easily becomes a kind of slogan. All this before ten o'clock, with a few jabs at his phone.

His Facebook entries often tell stories about the work he's undertaking as a life coach. They are both expository and inspirational. One entry reads:

The director of the CUNY Black Male Initiative invited us to present for all the CUNY schools. I asked him curiously as to why we got the invite. He said, "Pervis, we get tons of proposals from many organizations. However, never have we been approached by two men of color teaching other men of color how to be whole." These things are a reminder to always choose purpose over popularity. Be Great!

Pretty sweet morning, his work executed solely by using his phone, while crouching over a cup of expensive coffee. Most independent life coaches have a measure of this kind of control over their days. Oddly, the life coaches consulted for this book rarely wanted to share information about their living circumstances, their hometown, even their favorite restaurants. They preferred the anonymity allowed by distance, the control that an agreed-upon time and date for client meetings over the phone offers them.

After the updates, Pervis is quite clear that the work does not stop. The whirlwind of self-motivation keeps him moving. "For the rest of the morning, I'm either prepping for client calls," he says, "or developing the Black Male Initiative that my partner and I are trying to get going at a local college. Right?"

What's involved during the late morning hours, that time that Pervis—he wants to be referred to as just Pervis—calls "prepping"? Lesson plans, curriculum review, rehearsing? "Reading mostly," Pervis says. "I'm trying to stimulate my thoughts, before I get to the clients and stir up theirs." He is moved by the same material that tends to affect his clients. He acknowledges this is a pattern that comes from his training as a Christian, where he used the Bible as inspiration, and he brought gospel with him to his learning. But he's broadened his reading somewhat recently. This morning he's reading *The Alchemist* by Paulo Coelho, a classic of personal-growth literature, and *How People Grow*, by Henry Cloud and John Townsend, a book on the connection between personal growth and Scripture. Those, followed by the Bible.

Yes, life coaches plan. They prep. But life coaching—one-on-one sessions with a trained individual, a person devoted to helping you improve your life—is also highly improvisational. It demands a flexible approach, which allows for changes from week to week, if not on the fly. "You have to be pretty fluid," Pervis says. "That's why it helps to read a lot. It's more busy than it probably seems. Some days, pitching for a program presentation feels like the most important component of the job. Other times, I can't wait to get past that, to my sessions with the clients."

A signed contract for ongoing group work can represent an essential part of building a career as a life coach. The importance of the programs that Pervis creates lies in the fact that they include more people, a wider audience, and so, when planned right, the sessions can be more easily duplicated, increasing volume of potential clients. A life coach must be a businessperson first. They must ensure their own financial survival, without throttling their audience with matters of cost. A good presentation brings on more clients, more work. Pervis is happy to work that end of the job, since it gets his message to young men who need the help. "We have a contract with the city universities of New York with our Black Male Initiative program, which we're calling Alchemic Solutions, where we are coaching young men of color in emotional intelligence."

"Emotional intelligence" sounds a little buzzwordy, doesn't it?

Pervis laughs. "We're teaching them how to develop an emotional lexicon and how to process their emotions. They need to express their hurt."

In connecting with clients, Pervis is part healer. Pitching classes afterward to school administrators, he's part hustler. Working with his partner, fellow life coach Jeffrey Ulysse, also in his early thirties, on the program to empower young men of color, using feedback from public-school teachers, he's a fully integrated professional. It's a broad dynamic of work— inspirational, emotional, pedagogical. He needs to do well by his various programs every day. They are his bread and butter.

His writing is another way of delivering his message to clients. His new book provides an income stream as well as forming the basis of the program he's building for young men of color. He self-published the book, which to his mind makes him more of an entrepreneur, not less. Most life coaches seem to claim "best-selling" as an adjective of choice for their books, when listed on their own web page. Pervis uses the term "internationally sold" on his books, which is a bit confounding. He's got a new one, with a pretty cool title.

"It's called *Surthrival Mode*," he says. "A book that teaches men how to deal with their emotional traumas by processing them." A car horn blares on the street behind him. "The book does the work I try to do as a coach and teacher, by navigating through barriers and enabling the client to show up in life and within their relationships."

It sounds a little like he's reading copy off the back cover of his own book just then. And the blurb doesn't tell much. I repeat the title—or at least what I took it to be over the low din of traffic. *Survival Mode.*

"No, no," he says. "I bridged 'thriving' and 'survival' together. I made a new word. *Surthrival.*" He pauses there. Lets it sink in. "*Surthrival Mode.* Yeah. Just a sec," he says to me. We're on the phone. He's walking, carrying his phone at his side. The street is all clatter and banging. I can hear him greet someone, excuse himself, at some doorway. He's arrived at a coffee shop. He quiets himself when he sits. It's nice to feel him settle.

"Pervis," I say, "please tell me that you don't walk around the city like this while you do your sessions." He's young; it seems possible. This sort of urban traipsing around might be a kind of "surthrival" mode in itself. "Tom"—he laughs—"of course not. I have to be very focused for my sessions with clients. I owe them that much."

EVERY LIFE COACH HAS a different habit when it comes to their clients. Some carry long lists of active clients to whom they speak at regular intervals. Once a week is typical. Once a month appears to be the outer edge of what's acceptable. Most calls are scheduled, often in big chunks of time in the evening or afternoon. It's not unusual for a life coach on the East Coast, like Pervis, to have clients in western time zones, making it easier to place calls late at night.

Availability is an absolute, but training clients to trust the schedule is essential too. "When you have six people who need to speak with you, you can't have them calling anytime they want to," Pervis says. It is a matter of maintaining focus and purpose in your communication. "Random calls can take things over, and pretty soon you aren't coaching anymore," he says. "You're just answering the phone."

To combat that possibility, Pervis doesn't cling to an hour-long format. He reserves several hours a week for his sessions. Like most of the other life coaches I spoke to, he purposely calls these meetings "sessions," and allows them to range from forty-five minutes to more than two hours. Same price either way. "I like to use the end of the day or early evening for my sessions," he says. "I don't ever stack them all up on one night." He currently carries a load of five to six clients, and calls this typical. "There's a natural limit," he says. "You can't just treat it as a matter of volume," he says.

Five to six clients, each averaging a session a week; most

clients are spoken to in the afternoon or evening. I have to ask him what he charges. It's always a difficult question, asking someone what they make. I expect some throat clearing, a little hemming and hawing. "What do you charge?" I blurt.

Pervis doesn't hesitate. He knows people are curious, that life coaches are still sometimes regarded as charlatans and confidence men. "I charge $350 a session," he says. He makes no apology. He and his partner are charging $1,800 for the group work in the city schools; if they can develop it into something regular, on contract, he knows this too could be a good income stream.

"I'm worth it, Tom," he says confidently.

At one point, I ask Pervis the same question I ask of all the coaches . . . I want to ask about giving advice. Pervis is savvy, quick-witted, and experienced at defining life coaching for others. I expect he might acknowledge that leading clients to form their own answers seems like it might be construed as a form of giving advice. I half expect he'll have a direct answer to my question: How do you know the best advice to give a client?

But in response, Pervis just makes a sound like "Nah." He's silent for a while. "I don't give advice."

"Never?"

"Rarely," he says, leaning back in his chair now. "I'm not there to provide answers for my clients."

Don't they want advice? Don't they ask?

"They learn not to," he says. "No life coach gives advice. I think the thing most coaches believe is that you have the best answer within you."

He pauses, then sips a drink. "I mean obviously I have thoughts and opinions of my own. I *could* give advice. Yeah. But ultimately a client is more empowered when they come up with an action or a resolution themselves. That's what coaching is about, unearthing the greatness and the power within."

"Within what?"

"The client," he replies.

Where did he learn that? The not-giving-advice thing. Do life coaches know this instinctively?

He thinks for a moment. "I'm a minister too," he says. "In that role, I might give advice based on Scripture, sure. But that's a different muscle. Coaching is a whole different matter. The answers aren't there when you sit down. I need to stir up the mind to find the answer."

Where did he learn this? Pervis didn't go to a program in

life coaching, and doesn't mention any specific training on his website. He answers, brave and bright. He's as earnest as an apple. "I have a degree in business administration, and I'm finishing my master's in psychology from Columbia," he says. "And I read a lot. I start and end every session with a question for the client. I might draw that question from any of these backgrounds. Life coaching isn't very old. The field is still developing. I've had life coaches myself. I asked constantly about the way they worked."

He goes on to note that life coaching is not an exact science, in the same way psychology is not an exact science, the same way therapy is not an exact science. "We're a diverse group, offering diverse perspectives and experiences. I think all coaches would agree that being a life coach is about coming to a place where your client is empowered. That is not therapy. I'm not a therapist. Because I'm not *treating* anyone."

Pervis thinks for a bit. "The thing about giving advice is: People are not monolithic. Situations are not monolithic. There are so many variables involved that to give a broad, homogenized piece of advice is a little dangerous. Life coaches work to know their clients best. You have to aim to make the client into your expertise. Better to help them develop the tools to figure it out themselves."

Pervis tells a story in an effort to create a case study of the work one of his clients is doing with his coaching. He won't breach confidences, but he wants to paint a picture. Who are you working with right now? How does a session work?

Pervis ponders for a hot minute. Then he speaks. "One kid I'm working with in the Black Male Initiative, he's a college student, and his major was computer science. He's Muslim and his family kinda sorta forced him into that major. Maybe I should say they *strongly encouraged* him to go into computer science. You know, the money thing, for sure," he says, referencing the parents' natural desire to prepare their child for the best career.

"This young man was very discouraged, very shut down, when it came to talking about academics," he says. "But it was clearly the issue at hand. Was he going to get through years of schooling studying a subject matter he didn't care about? He was depressed and considering dropping out."

As usual, Pervis opened the session—this was in a group setting—with a question. But instead of asking the expected question—"What do you want to get out of your education?"—Pervis came at the matter tangentially. He asked: What is your passion? Where is your joy? At first, the student couldn't define his passion. He certainly couldn't connect education to joy. But Pervis pushed him to think about it literally. To use his mind to locate where he felt happiest. He asked the student to think about a map of the campus. Where did he feel something like passion? In what building did he sense anything like joy? By creating a physical setting, the young man found that he felt the rumblings of passion in his desire to understand the human mind, and the workings of his own mind. Psychology classes, though he took them mostly as electives, did this. In those classes, he was excited enough to argue for his positions. This, then, was his passion. He named it that first day. He located his joy in psychology and in the tissue of historical understanding he found in his art history classes.

"And so, within the first two sessions he shared all that," Pervis said. "And by the third session, he switched his major from computer science to psychology and art history. And it's changed how he thinks of himself. His demeanor's changed, the way he's showing up has changed. He's shown up to every single session. He's very vocal. He's been consistent. We originally thought that he would be the one that would kind of flake out on us."

I remind Pervis that it's easy to imagine that the young man's parents might not be happy with the change.

Pervis smiles. "A life coach works for the client alone," he says. "The client made his own decision and that means something. We all want autonomy, and maybe that's what he drew from this [work] most of all. I have to think his parents see that."

Pervis puts me in touch with a longtime client, actress Lisa Nicole Carson, forty-nine, who now identifies as a mental health advocate in Los Angeles. Costar of the hit shows *Ally McBeal* and *ER* in the late nineties, she saw her career derailed when, shortly after being diagnosed with bipolar disorder, she suffered several humiliating public breakdowns at work-related events in Los Angeles. She famously disappeared from her professional life in the years that followed.

For seven years Pervis worked with her to understand and control her condition, and to set about reviving her once-promising career. "I was living in the shadows, in darkness, and living in shame," she says. "I had been humiliated by everyone, peers, the press, everything. And it took me a long time to even process what had happened to me."

While still in that state, she met Pervis at a birthday party, and he informally listened to her story. When he called, and came back for more listening, she found that he was encouraging her to take on the one thing she feared most. "*People* magazine had been pursuing me for seven or eight years. And I had been dodging them pretty gracefully the whole time. But Pervis told me to stop treating it like they were chasing me, and to not dodge them anymore. He asked me, 'What if you treat that like an opportunity instead?' He turned it all around for me."

At the time, being bipolar was not a condition that was much talked about openly. "I'd never had therapy. Pervis was the first person who got me to see that I could really get started, really work to get my career going again, to come out of the shadows. That was Pervis."

Carson still speaks to Pervis periodically. She's begun to get roles again, after a ten-year absence from television. Working with a life coach turned her toward asking productive questions about herself, she says. Pervis opens doors to change, she says, by dealing with who she is as a person, rather than a patient. "I'd say if you don't want a clinical, spacey, distant overview on your life, and if you don't want your pain to control you, it might be good to get in touch with a life coach, one like Pervis. He's a listener. He makes me look at my life again and again. Somehow, he's taught me how to plan for what I cannot control. That's something that never seemed possible to me. That's made me live."

When Pervis thinks of his current clients, he seems to flip through a list in his head. This act makes him smile. They are young people, making the same mistakes previous generations have made. "Last week, I had a client, so she basically, I guess . . . I'm trying to think of the right word," he says, before wisely skipping the nomenclature. "She's great, a brilliant young lady, twenty-three years old, but, she's used to getting by on her looks, scamming and using men to pay her bills and things like that, hustling in that way, and now she's realizing she feels just empty."

Pervis says his goal is to get this young woman to a place where she's not a victim. A place where she can see that life happens because of her, as a consequence of her actions, rather than as a punishment for them. He does this by posing a question about changing the way she uses language. "She was spending most of her sessions talking about what this person did, what this person did, what this person did, and I had to stop her and tell her, I don't care about what they do. I'm focused on you. What if the only thing you talked about was you? Like every sentence?"

He was working to get her from a place where she was

constantly pointing the finger at everybody else to one where she started to take responsibility for her role in what happened to her. "Concentrating on her own actions gave her the ability to create the life that she wants for herself," he says. "It gave her the pen to write the narrative of her life."

Do potential clients find the fact of his religious faith troublesome? Do they worry they are hiring a minister rather than a coach? Do they resist?

Pervis breathes a little. Some don't like it at first. It doesn't take them long to figure him out. "I don't even have to say anything," he says. "They're like 'Oh my God. You're religious. I can tell that you're Christian!'"

That's when he explains the job of a life coach. A life coach is not a minister, he tells them. A minister might have a set of answers. Pervis tells them: I do not provide answers as a coach. "Even so," he says to me over the phone, "some answers are common to all of us."

He's asked to name one. What's an answer that speaks to each one of us? He takes another deep breath, then starts in with what he knows.

"Well, everybody wants to be whole. Everybody wants to understand why they're here," Pervis says. "Everybody wants to thrive, wants to understand the meaning of who they are. Everybody wants to know that they're loved, to know they matter, that they're seen and heard. I know these things as a life coach, as a man, and as a minister. But in my work, I answer as a life coach."

Meaning what?

"People just have to be asked the right questions," he says. And then he is quiet, thinking, percolating the very question that will help me most in the moment to come.

2

NOT A MENTOR

Farrell Reynolds, 76
Woodstock, NY

The town of Woodstock, New York, sits in a somehow luminous crook in the road, forty-three miles from the farm where the epic concert of concerts was held in 1969. It's a burg. A hamlet. A hippie spirit still grips the place, a spirit evident in the contrast between the somnambulant pace of the locals and the urgent comings and goings of the weekenders, those who wish to relocate or retire from New York City, and the tourists who follow—bird watchers, history buffs, bicyclists. They come for the quality of the food, the music, the local crafts—represented in the skein of posters advertising yoga classes, acupressure discussion groups, Ayurvedic healing seminars, and pancake suppers that rings the telephone poles along the main road.

It is in Woodstock where you might encounter Farrell Reynolds, the retired communications exec. He's a tall man, with white hair, kind blue eyes, and an impish grin.

Farrell Reynolds is a certified executive coach, an early graduate of the program at Coach U. He's a certified life coach with extensive training. Furthermore, he's seventy-six years old. Old. And he does absolutely no work branding himself, and very little in selling his services through social media, advertising, or self-promotion. The thought of it makes him a little sick. He's a word-of-mouth guy who doesn't much like the term "life coach" at all. Reynolds had a successful first career in television ad sales, and beyond. He has an established corporate clientele, and a growing group of clients who seek him out because he's wizened, witty, and a little impatient. He's also experienced, as his work record shows.

Farrell Reynolds walked the path of a generation of executives who launched their careers in the seventies. Even he might call the members of his cohort "Old White Guys." He was a naval officer for four years after graduating from Manhattan College. Then he worked for IBM for a couple of years before getting into the television business, selling commercial time to local and national advertisers.

"Working at various and sundry television stations, and networks, that was actually the core of what I did for the next thirty-five years," he says by phone. Always by phone with the life coaches. He spent ten years at Turner Broadcasting, from 1980 to 1990, and during the last three years he was president of the network's sales organization. He started training as an executive coach in his last days as a television executive, including participation in some of the first classes at Coach U, where he gained certification in the late nineties. He carried on as a freelancer after he moved to Woodstock in the early 2000s.

Asked whether he considers himself an executive coach or a life coach now, Reynolds pauses before speaking. "Well . . . a life coach. Hmm. First of all, to my mind, that's way too broad a description." He wants me to imagine the process that someone who ends up calling himself a life coach goes through before finally recognizing himself as such. "A person says, 'I need a life coach.' And someone steps up. A life coach. But everything starts with a declaration from the client. 'I'm a mess. Help me.'

"Well, all right, if that's what a life coach responds to, that's fine. I would say people of a clerical persuasion—not clerks, but religious clerical—would lean into that. And the others are already out there. Life coaches could be psychiatrists, psychologists would be life coaches, social workers would be life coaches, so on and so forth. So a life coach is someone that thinks they can provide the same service and doesn't have to go through all of the hassle of getting a license or spending five years in a seminary or whatever, and it just opens the doors to just a lot of ineffective help."

But Reynolds presses on, rephrases the problem. "'Life coach' is way too broad. Yeah. I know that there are people who take coaching courses, and then they're encouraged in these coaching courses to be broad in their interests. But I also know the [course] I took twenty years ago encouraged us to develop a narrow area of interest. A focus. Coach to the specifics of life, not to life itself. Be a coach to a massage therapist. Be a coach to accountants. Be a coach to bartenders. Be a coach to retail workers. Be a coach to service personnel. *Whatever.* But a life coach? Maybe it has a certain cachet now, but for me, it sort of gets my bullshit buzzer going."

He pauses then. "I'm a coach to executives, to answer your question."

Reynolds realizes this answer in itself might push certain

buttons. "I don't mean that in a negative way. It seems to me if someone is looking for a life coach, it means they haven't really developed a focus on what their problem is, what their barrier is, where they stumble. And this really means they haven't done the work. They have to do the work themselves."

AS AN EXECUTIVE COACH, Reynolds often leans on rules he learned from his time in business, and combines them with techniques for rethinking and reinventing his own lexicon for business, techniques that he learned at Coach U. He's different from a typical life coach, who concentrates less on the outcome than on the manner in which decisions are reached. Reynolds plainly acts as someone who's been there before. His technique as coach is to give the client the mind-set to act effectively, because by the time clients get to Reynolds, they likely have the skills they need to do the job.

Still, he has his limits. For instance, the time he gives his clients as their executive coach is circumscribed. Early on, he tells his clients: Eight weeks. One session a week. He generally assigns one exercise per session, a different exercise for each client. The exercises are sent to the client by e-mail between sessions.

Why limit the number of sessions? "You have to make time valuable. So I make their time with me scarce."

Reynolds started at Coach U over twenty years ago. While Coach University is the birthplace of standardized life-coach training, it's not a school per se. There is no campus, no permanent faculty or fixed curriculum. There is no way that this for-profit program could be considered an alma mater for Reynolds. He has drifted a little.

What does he recall about the course at Coach U? "It was about six months long; I never went anywhere. It was a telephone course. We called in and there were two dozen people on the line." Note: not *online*. *On the line*. One marathon phone call. "It could be chaotic," Reynolds allows. He's sure that has changed. "Computers"—he sniffs—"weren't really all that 'in' at the time."

There was a leader on every call, a coach leader. And he remembers the presence of a dean of coaching or a president coach. But he no longer remembers names. Reynolds does remember the previously mentioned Thomas Leonard, author of *The Portable Coach* and founder of Coach U. I remind him of Leonard's name. Reynolds was sometimes in on the calls. Reynolds found Leonard's writings brilliant, and he went deep into Leonard's mode of thinking. When

Leonard died, Reynolds was on the phone, in the middle of a class. "I don't know if Leonard left any legacy there," he says now, "but he was remarkable. I still have his workbook someplace. It was focused, and very, very structured, and somewhat narrow, which is a good thing."

Limiting things, narrowing your focus, is an important element of coaching for Reynolds. He favors small discoveries over all-encompassing truths, and uses exercises that help the executives he's working with reinvent value and perspective. "The best work I can do is connecting to the needs of the people who hire me," he says. "I speak their language. I've faced their problems. I keep them in my sights. When what I do works, they will connect other clients to me. That's the business model. One executive at a time."

When asked about who he works with, these executives . . . are they always at the top of the command chain, or does he sometimes work with lower-tier salesmen? . . . Reynolds pshaws. Then he's quiet. Then he sniffs. "Okay. I'll give you my latest client.

"This is a fellow who I know who's very entrepreneurial in his approach. He's a high-level guy, in telecommunications. Not the very top, but senior level." Reynolds knew the guy wanted to be coached, because at first he'd call and say something like, "Let's get together and shoot the breeze." A phrase that Reynolds knew to mean that he wanted to pick Reynolds's brain, at no cost. "He called every two months," Reynolds relates, "and the message he was giving me was: I want to form a relationship with you, at my convenience. So then I confronted it. I needed to start the coaching. I always draw limits on the coaching relationship and the time I will spend giving over to it. A coach has to have limits. Either you have value as a coach or you don't. A good coach has to believe he or she does [have value]."

You can't give it away. That makes sense. A life coach places value on the conventional exchanges of the everyday world, on conversation that might otherwise go unnoticed. A coach can't allow herself to be duped into coaching. There has to be a limit that marks where the coaching begins.

Interestingly, Reynolds draws other sorts of limits on the relationship. He curtails the time he spends with clients and dictates the manner in which meetings will take place. He will declare to clients: "Okay, here's what that relationship will look like. We will meet for one hour, for eight weeks. I name my fee. And I tell them I'd rather do meetings on the phone than in person."

Does he ever meet with resistance from executives who

are paying top dollar for his coaching? Don't they expect his personal attention? "I tell them: I'm the coach. Believe me, it's better to do it on the phone."

When asked to elaborate, Reynolds asserts that there's an overarching set of circumstances quite common among people in business. The workings of corporations can be secretive. These clients want to tell stories; they want to trade on that. They want to expound. "As a coach," he says, "you have to strip that away. So, you tell them: use the phone.

"I don't need to know their relationship with their father, or their first boss, et cetera, et cetera. I don't mean to be demeaning to my clients, I just don't need to know that. And also, they have to remember: I'm not their friend. I'm definitely on their side, but I'm not on the friend wavelength. The distance provided by the phone cuts out the bullshit factor of a power lunch."

REYNOLDS KNOWS THAT MOST coaches—whether credentialed or not—start their work with clients by using a form of self-assessment. What tool does he use?

"I do several exercises," he says. "First I want to be sure

that my responses and input are reaching my client, so I always ask them to critique every session a little bit. Their ability to evaluate talent is fundamental to their station in management. So, I turn the tables. 'Was there something I missed? Is there something that is not resonating with you?'"

He wants that part done quickly. He pushes things, because he does not want to spend another half hour critiquing the session. "Time has value, after all." Reynolds's demeanor is proof that a person can't be afraid of candid evaluation within a corporate structure so long as it leads to more productive action.

He leans into the next part of his answer, which is the exercise he was asked about. Reynolds pushes his executives, using the tools of a corporate manager as tools of direct self-assessment. "Recently I asked a client to create a budget."

What sort of budget?

"Not a time budget, not a fiscal budget," he says. "My client was whining about the needs of his family, his adult children and his wife, and questioned if they valued him as he felt they should. He had that all backward. He should have been thinking about himself, not others." Reynolds pauses then, and takes a breath. He's out of the executive realm, into the behavior of the individual, the purview of a life coach. "He needed to reflect on how *he* did things," he says. "You can always blame people, but you can't necessarily change them. So I spoke to him directly as a CEO. Show me the numbers. I told him, make me a document. Create a budget as to how you dispense your affections."

This is a language the client spoke, Reynolds asserts. It ought to come easily to long-term executives. "I said: 'I'm not going to explain it any further. That's it, that's the assignment. Not how you should or could disperse your affection. Just look at yourself and assess. Nothing more to it.'"

There was resistance. But eventually the executive accepted the task. Then Reynolds asked him to fax the document, to e-mail it. In his work life, Reynolds always wants a hard copy in his hands. "I mean, it's a budget," he says. "I don't want a story; I don't need a verbal recitation. Creativity can reveal itself in numbers too."

The budget was a beautiful thing too. "The client understood the tool because he had used it all his life in decision making," Reynolds says. "It made him aware of certain deficits he hadn't seen before. And I think he saw where he was spending too little. And where he's committed to too much."

Just numbers. In columns.

"Just a budget," Reynolds says, "but he knew how to look at that as work, how to address his spending dispassionately rather than assigning an outsized emotional import to affection."

Reynolds speaks regularly about knowing your product, the message of selling. He doesn't want to replace, or reinvent, the lexicon of business. He doesn't want to create new tools. Instead he uses the language of business radically, making it a tool of self-reflection. This is where he stands alone, how he distinguishes himself. "I'm immensely grateful for having that business mind-set," he says. "That was not the way I was throughout a lot of my life; I didn't appreciate the tools I was using."

REYNOLDS LIVES HOURS FROM the city. He's available mostly by cell phone. His website speaks starkly about his methods. He does very little self-promotion and very little social media promotion. There's a Facebook page somewhere, he says. But he can't seem to remember where. "Someone either knows who I am, what I've done for other executives or what I did for decades in television ad sales, or they don't. My social media is my reputation, that's the connection to others, the authority I need with others." Plainly, he's not an internet guy. He has a website, but claims he hasn't looked at it in years.

It's still out there, he is told. I looked at it the week before I contacted him. It does appear pretty untouched. Reynolds asks how someone can tell that. The site just doesn't communicate much information, he is told. You don't seem to be selling yourself.

He grunts in displeasure at the thought. He is asked: So, *not* selling yourself, that's purposeful?

"It's not lazy," he answers. "If someone hears of me, or knows me, and they want to talk, then I'm here. Why would I put any energy into selling myself?"

If not yourself, then what are you selling?

He is selling his thinking, he says. His ability to connect thinking about business to reflecting upon life, to looking at business as units of life. "In a lot of ways, I'm selling my Four Rules of Business," Reynolds says.

But the world is always presenting lists of rules; surely that can't be the limit of his work. Where does the coaching come in? How do these rules register with the clients?

"Everything comes with an exercise," he says. "My clients

know—*write it all down*. These tasks define the rules in terms they can see. In business, your work defines everything."

FARRELL REYNOLDS'S
FOUR RULES OF BUSINESS

EARLY ON, I SAY to my clients: "Okay, here's what we do." And then I always lay out these four elements of business as I know them.

Rule One: Know your market. People always say, well, if I know anything, I know my market. So I make them assess: tell me about your market. And usually what happens is when they start in it becomes apparent. They really don't know. There are gaps and presumptions. Maybe they really don't know how their product is used, or what the need of their marketplace is, so on and so forth. So I ask them to just write a paragraph and send it to me, about what their market is like. Keep it to a paragraph. This is a challenge for people who think they know everything about their business. And listen, it's not like I'm a genius here. I came up with these four elements because I knew that I didn't know them when I was working. They were my deficits too.

Rule Two: Know your product. And they would say again, "Oh, I truly know my product." And I'll say, "Well, I'm sure you do from a mechanical point of view, but you also have to know how adaptable your product is, how your product can be used." I ask, "What's the plasticity involved in the experience of your product?" And that gets people thinking, and actually it's a very creative exercise for my clients. I say: "Write a report on this, as if you just discovered the product." They get in, they see there's more to their product than they ever thought.

Rule Three: Know the appetites of the market and how your product satisfies them. This is a nuanced, but very important aspect of the business of all corporations, and boy, I learned this with start-ups, and timing, these start-ups are all internet-based, and I would ask these young, bright code writers and computer scientists, "Talk to me about the user interface." And I could see the thought bubbles over their heads. "What the fuck is he talking about?" They never took into account what's the user experience. What's going on on the other side of the screen? For them it was all about the capabilities of the written code rather than the experience of the product itself. So, write me a memo defining your product like I've never seen it before.

Rule Four: Continually redefine how you inform the marketplace of this product. This stuff moves fast. If you don't do it, it will be too late, and the ability to inform customers will be lost. And this gets into the marketing aspect of their whole business cycle. So what have you done recently? What will you do tomorrow? Write it out. Make a list. Send that to me.

And when I lay that out, those four points, and maybe we're on the phone, maybe we meet in a restaurant, I'm narrowing their focus to some basic discoveries. Narrow the focus.

ANY COACH WILL STATE they must stay detached from the performance of their clients. When Reynolds is coaching executives, he maintains that he has no stake in the outcome for the company. The individual client exists autonomously. So the coach makes rules and crafts assignments; they reinvent the work they are already doing—the reports, the proposals, the forecasts and budgets. These documents allow clients to translate their coaching work into what they do in their jobs themselves. "I don't work for their company,"

Reynolds says. "I don't work above the client. I work *for* them. I'm not being paid to teach the job."

Is it something like being a mentor, then?

Reynolds shakes that off. "For a long time people told me: this is a mentorship business. But the truth is, I'm just a set of ideas. I can't find anything worthwhile in selling my presence. I'm not going to work on display for others." He's clearly been down this road before. A life coach has to set limits.

"I'm not a part of the corporate organization," he says. "So I'm damned sure not a mentor." Reynolds is a contrary force of nature.

Reynolds doesn't see himself as everyman. He's a person who can recognize what people are doing dispassionately. He recognizes behavior first, and separates it from good intentions. "I see bad habits," he says. "I have them too. I know exactly what my clients are doing."

What would be his bad habit? His worst.

"Thinking too much," he says immediately. "That's something I used to be guilty of. Sometimes we get much more satisfaction from mulling over a problem in our head rather than taking steps to solve it. Your head, first of all, is a very safe place. Action is much harder. You have to be ready to act."

One tool he learned to look at critically? The relative importance of various measures of time in business. Everybody in the world thinks of a year as fifty-two weeks. But time works differently in business. The calendar itself operates in its own fashion in different departments. Thirteen weeks means more to a salesman than a full year. Thirteen weeks, a single quarter, represents the next benchmark, the next set of goals, and commissions, not to mention it marks ground zero for the quarter that follows. In sales, the accounting system is based on quarters. "But those weeks, they are just one unit for a salesman," he says. "They are just as good as one day."

Much of the work of a life coach lies in measuring the perceptions of one person against the dynamics of a larger group. Often the life coach helps deconstruct assumptions about how the world works. Every component of a given business, every department, brings the culture of its own calendar to the table.

Reynolds knows from his experience as a sales executive that, for a salesman, thirteen weeks is merely one sales period. Sales, he says, is mostly relationships and patterns of response. "Relationships aren't developed in one thirteen-week time unit; trust isn't developed in thirteen weeks. Recognizing a problem takes more than thirteen weeks; creating a solution doesn't happen in thirteen weeks," he says. He's had to teach executives to understand how time functions for salesmen as opposed to production staff, to teach them the relative power of time.

"This is really a lesson for management," Reynolds says, "more than the individual salesperson. Time is different for everyone. Just don't think you're motivating your sales force or your sales managers by hanging this sword of Damocles over their head and stating: 'If you don't make the fucking budget in the next thirteen weeks, you're all gone.' These threats don't work. That thirteen weeks is their tool. Don't make them use their own tools against themselves."

FARRELL REYNOLDS BREATHES DEEPLY after we discuss how these formulations impact executives who haven't been in a classroom for decades. "First thing I do in a session is make their task small, basic, because I want them to be free to reflect.

"They're used to massive jobs, with a lot of synthesis of facts. So I make them concentrate on a single small action." Then he adds, "That's it in a nutshell. That's the basis of everything I do.

"And there's just one other thing," he says, "on this life coaching. Remember, I don't do this for a living."

I wait for the rest of this. And . . . ?

"Most life coaches—and this is not a criticism, it's just a very real observation—they do it for a living. So their screen, their filter, is not as fine as mine. They put up with a lot more than I would."

And because of their own bottom line, coaches can't turn away potential clients. "I mean you're not prone to," he says. "The more clients you have, with their own situations, the more answers you have to have. The more formulations. The focus gets broad."

Narrow your focus.

"Right," Reynolds says. "Right."

"Is that your main rule for life coaching?"

He thinks for a moment. "Yes," he says. But then he releases a Gatling gun of assertions that any life coach has to remember. "A life coach should end every phone conversation with the question: How has this met your expectations and your needs? The life coach should want to know. I do. Clarity. I'm not making a puzzle for them. I'm trying to free them of puzzles. Clarity. I mean, how much could you do if you could be clear about everything?"

And just like that, we end with his question.

3

NOT A TEACHER

Amy Moser, 50
London, England

I t's easy to see how adept good coaches are at listening to, and connecting with, their clients. These clients tend to be adults, caught at moments of crisis—acute or chronic— which might range from a professional crisis to a relationship crisis to an existential crisis. And these clients are most often reaching out for help. They are willing. They are buying.

But what about life coaches who seek to reach an audience that hasn't previously been included in a traditional life-coaching target group before? Can life coaching be reinvented for others?

A decade and a half ago, Amy Moser found herself mid-career in corporate communications, living in London, working at a human resources consulting firm. There came a moment when her supervisor had a nervous breakdown, and Moser was forced to take over the department. She was wary of the demands of the new position, and worried that she didn't have the resources to handle the job any better than her boss had. She needed a little help.

"There was a guy in HR whose wife had started doing this coaching," she says. "I thought, Okay, I need some help. I'll get coached by her, though I had no idea what I was undertaking."

Moser expected to have an experience of personal therapy, in which she might, for example, relate war stories from the office to someone who would in turn provide coping strategies for dealing with an unresponsive colleague or uninspired staff or the new heavier load of paperwork she faced. She'd gone for counseling during her life in the States. Now, instead of psychotherapy, she found that life coaching was something else entirely. It changed her attitude toward work. It changed her energy level. It convinced her that she had the tools to do a bigger job than she'd ever expected to find herself in. She was surprised to find that it changed . . . well, her mind.

Moser is a careful listener, willing to wait out the delays of transatlantic communication. She's used to working with skeptical clients, on the phone and in person. After years in communications positions, she's developed an interest in dealing with interpersonal issues in the workplace. She long sensed that if workers were happier, a workplace could reinvent itself quite easily. But she'd never found the right tools before. Once she had some coaching under her belt, she hooked into her life's calling—working to help people reengineer themselves for the better. Concentrating on people rather than on the power structure of the offices they worked in.

"The exercises and techniques the coach exposed me to were entirely new to me. Using the coaching, I was able to create a more positive mind-set for myself. I worked more than I ever had and I enjoyed work more than ever." Moser speaks from the office of her own coaching business in London, a blank wall behind her, with the top of a clothes hamper just visible. Her office is an extra room in her home, as it is for nearly every coach interviewed here. A couple of them didn't have offices at all.

But Moser's not apologetic about her surroundings. Why should she be? The work of a life coach starts with connecting to people. Office settings have very little to do with it.

"I'd had some therapy in the States, and I'd continued to do some work with group therapy in the UK because I'm just into that; I learn from it. But life coaching was different in that it was really more about my future." There was a lot to consider in her past too. She'd transplanted herself in her early thirties, from the States to the UK. Her parents were aging, her college friends slipping into the shadows. But she had plenty to think about in her future too. She was starting a family, moving up the ladder at work, grappling with living in London, one of the most expensive cities in the world. "With coaching, I wasn't going back into my past, looking at stuff and why it all happened." She began looking forward to discoveries in her coaching sessions, which were about the now, the moment she was living in. And the moment to come. "The coaching I got was more about my path to solutions, and about what was going to happen in the future to me. For me. I liked that."

Early on, the coach working with Moser suggested she take a course in coaching herself, that it might help in Moser's handling of internal communications at her job. Coaching, and coach training, translates into clients, and what with training sessions sometimes as short as a week, a certified life coach can begin work after as little as six months of training; uncertified coaches can begin even sooner. The various levels of certification (there are many) allow for more training over the years. "My coach told me that learning to coach just might help *me* in general with life," she said.

Moser was jazzed. As is common for company-based coaching programs, her department head actually sponsored her course work as a continuing education effort. "While I was working there, I got my first NLP qualification, and the title neuro-linguistic practitioner within the first year." Moser had been drawn to neuro-linguistic programming, a key component of the certification process of the International Coach Federation, and begun training in it. In the UK, she continued this training even as she moved on to a new job at the BBC.

Once that started, it became clear that Moser's work wasn't finished. Suddenly she was in the coaching game, and she was still being coached herself. Life coaching is an inclusive field. It doesn't exist in a top-down, teacher-student dynamic. The dynamic goes two ways, from teacher to student and from student to teacher.

Moser swears by this reciprocal process. "The foundation of any coach training has always been that you should experience it yourself," she says now. "You have to be open enough to want to do it as much, or more than, the person being coached." It's as easy to resist the help of a coworker as it is to accept it. Trust is always an issue, especially when one worker is promoting a work-based program for the other. There's a natural skepticism. Moser's interest in personality dynamics made her a natural. What connected her to others was her interest in their humanity outside the workplace as well as in it. "When I started, the big point was: You're not here to learn to be a coach completely," she says. "You're also here to be coached. That stayed with me as a principle of the field: I always am being coached by somebody else."

THE TERM "NEURO-LINGUISTIC PROGRAMMING" sounds a little too much like a plot point from a bad *Star Trek* episode, but there is a kind of energy and optimism underpinning the field. This energy has stayed with Moser, as coach and client. NLP changed her, as a nascent coach, in her attitude and sense of herself. Lots of the work comes from the way we naturally employ language. "There's an NLP concept about moving *toward* a future state as opposed to away from it. 'Away from' means you get into problem focus. The issue that's stopping you from getting a better outcome is the problem focus. I move toward things now. That's the point you start to say things like: 'I can't do it. I don't know how. I don't know what to do next.'"

Moser learned to lean forward, from the way she performed at work and from what she learned as a mother. "I found that I responded to the way NLP leans. *Toward*. And toward is typified by 'I want' and 'I'm going to' and 'This is my next step' kind of thing." She pauses then, waiting in thought. "So a lot of it is kind of creative thinking that helps people get unstuck from patterns that are holding them back."

A skeptic might say that this does not seem creative. It seems like we're using corporate lingo instead of the language we use in the everyday. "That's a good way of thinking about it," she says. "Maybe it's not creative. I guess it's more like *reinventing* the way you use language as a cue to your brain."

Look at the last sentence of the last paragraph again. In this very answer, Amy Moser is leaning toward acknowledgment and change. She is *leaning toward* the part of the answer that indicates insight and productivity.

Moser is on her own among the life coaches profiled in these pages in her enthusiasm for NLP. She has none of the fiery attitude of Farrell Reynolds, even less of the spiritual conviction of Pervis Taylor. Her brand of coaching is simply a more sedate, less provocative manner of doing business with yourself. Moser has a scholarly interest in methods of communication and the articulation of the self. She uses coaching to put these methods into action. She is a kind of researcher, a data collector. Careful and precise in the manner in which she approaches her work and her coaching.

A central proposition of NLP is that our brain gets trapped in neurological habits that prevent us from changing basic outcomes in our life. Moser enjoys considering the way we hold ourselves back from outcomes that will be beneficial to us. "I see change in the way people assess themselves. The words they use to describe where they are," she says. "I'll go in to run an idea by a department manager, and ask him to track his assessment of an upcoming project. Rate the outcome on a scale from one to ten. He might say, 'Right now I'm a three out of ten.' He'll then talk about the outcome he fears, the failure represented by three out of ten, rather than what he is after: a change. My training as a coach means I'll be sitting there thinking how do I get him to a five out of ten, but if he doesn't want to do that, then maybe we should try something else."

What are the other tools? What else did NLP put at your disposal? I ask her.

"I ask people to write a lot," she says. "This gives them their own structures, their own starting points. I have a kind of list of questions that I ask a client on the first meeting that help me assess where they are now. Later I ask them the questions again. I also use a coaching contract, which is just a really short one-pager that I use to help clients understand where I'm coming from. A lot of this is my own stuff. I'm just outlining the principles of what I do and how we're going to work together." This was all fine for in-house corporate training, but eventually, when Moser had school-age children, her interests broadened. She began to look for ways that life coaching might benefit children. She took her tools into the London school system. The questions are simple. What are these kids working on? What are their issues? What outcomes are they after?

One of the central issues is testing pressure. "In the UK, young kids have to be pretty achievement oriented," she says. "They take a lot of exams. When they're eleven, they take an exam to get into senior school. They have to be interviewed as well. I think there's a lot of pressure on them to perform at this age. A lot of them simply need more confidence when it comes to getting around these moments."

Teenagers face similar pressures. The UK uses a battery of tests called the A-levels to identify university-bound students. These tests are more comprehensive than those in the United States, and more competitive. Moser acknowledges that British high schoolers have to make more decisions about what they want to do at an earlier age than Americans.

When I asked her about how the children view her role in the after-school program, she shrugged. It's very matter-of-fact. "I coach them, yes. And when I go in there, my hope is that I'm another one of the teachers that comes in to work with them after school on different things, like the ballet teacher, the piano teacher, or the speech-coach person. I'm the life teacher, I guess," she says, "but I'm not a teacher. There are no test scores. No report cards. I want them to develop tools to deal with life. I want them to take these tools along with them. They learn their own lessons. I'm trying to teach them how to continue doing that for themselves."

And how will that happen? I wonder. She's asking the students to be resourceful, unafraid, thoughtful. All of them can do it, she says. Through life coaching, she hands out the tools—the right questions to ask oneself under pressure, the right ways to reprogram their answers so they can reveal who they are, rather than hide it. Language. Frankness. Reflection. These are the tools of a life coach; Amy Moser is simply handing them out earlier than other coaches, to an audience that is hungry for them. "I'm really not a teacher. I want *them* to set the agenda," she says. "The coaching is about *their* change. I don't talk about myself."

This is another point all life coaches make: they don't talk about themselves. Moser remembers that at first, doing this was hard, but it was necessary, no matter how young the clients. "A coach maintains a kind of neutrality when working with any client, but especially children. It's got to be about them." And the outcome she describes is the same one that every other life coach describes for his or her clients, no matter what their age. "I want them to find the answer themselves," she says. "I want them to find the resources that they're going to keep using for the rest of their life because they found the answer by themselves."

A life coach has to make a living. Moser works in London, using her life-coach earnings as her primary revenue stream. So naturally, the income question comes up. Moser hedges slightly. The one-on-one work is more lucrative, to be sure, than the group work, but she wants to reach as many students as possible. "I'm dealing with the parents, who are paying for these things, coming in. They know the score. For instance, I've got a new client whom I'm going to meet in a few minutes after I leave here. Her parents agreed we'll do five sessions for a package of six hundred pounds."

She's enthusiastic about the program she's attached to: Helping Kids. "I have a relationship with the school where I'm doing work with the teachers, presentations for the parents, and sessions with the students in small groups. That's kind of like my business model, which I'm constantly refining."

She asks what other coaches are charging for the work they do. The coaches in the States report fees averaging around $350 per session.

The answer stuns her a little. "Per *session*?" She sighs. "My God."

Most of these coaches are heavily into social media, she's told. Their individual coaching often takes place over the phone.

Moser shrugs. Being present in the room feels like a real advantage when it comes to coaching young students. "I've done a few clients where I've been on Skype or on social media, but most of my clients are local, so that's a different matter. I'd prefer to be here, with them."

She admits that perhaps she isn't diligent enough about making herself known to a larger market. "I rely a lot on the branding of Helping Kids. We merge our presentations, and often do our presentations side by side. We do that sort of work together. So I lean on that. I have to say, it's hard for me to go out there and sell myself to people by saying, 'Here are my credentials.' I believe a bit too much in word of mouth."

When asked what makes her different from other life coaches, Moser thinks for a moment, then cites her background as a communications specialist and her passion for lab science during her college years, her writing ability. "The coaching I do is more about coming up with solutions, and even making a record," she says. "I really want that. I write notes after every session. Most coaches don't, but I write a one-and-a-half or two-page note after every session. I work to give the client an overview of what I did, while noting the techniques."

She admits that these notes are as much for her as they are for the client. At the very least they provide her with a valuable record. Although she leans forward in her thinking and reflection, as per her NLP training, there are also times when she looks back. "A lot of times," she says, "I need to go through the steps again, or I want to have the client do that, so they can get them right, practice, and use them again. That's why the record matters."

It is late afternoon in London. Moser has to go. She gathers her things, pulling her purse from under a desk. She's about to set out into the world. She pats a pile of the files she keeps, and stands. "These records are the tools of change and the things I teach. That's why I write them up. If nothing else, they're what goes home with the parents. That's where change will occur with these kids. Coaching has to go beyond the relationship with the coach."

So why not feature that in her self-promotion? Why not sell that? Moser laughs a little. There are only so many hours, she says. She has a Facebook page, and a separate web page with testimonials from clients, but she doesn't tune these up on a daily basis like Pervis Taylor or Markita Collins does. "I just don't use that stuff very well," she says, sounding resigned.

It would seem, at this moment, that life coach Amy Moser is doing the *away-from* thing with her language. Told that she is leaning *away from* the change rather than toward it, she laughs and acknowledges the truth of this. "Pretty good observation," she says. "You would make a good coach yourself."

Talk to a coach long enough, and the lessons become yours:

Lean toward something. Onward. Another generation of coaches always awaits.

4

NOT A FRIEND

Gregory Diehl, 30
The Philippines, currently

Some people see life coaching as the warm and fuzzy frontier of the affirmation business. The coaches we've encountered so far could be considered friendly and caring; they navigate the space around personal relationships without great risk because their attentions are gentle and unforced. Yes, they are working to tip over reinforcement patterns in order to trigger change in their clients, but they are attentive, caring, and funny in doing so. They seek to connect.

Most of us have encountered athletic coaches—football, tennis, hockey—who didn't care about connection. They were not interested in making their athletes feel good about what they brought with them to the job. They yelled, they belittled, they demanded that the athletes dig deeper and produce more. And they pretended not to care if the athletes didn't respond. Except for yelling. That just made them yell louder. But what about life coaches? Can they work with paying clients while provoking, antagonizing, and upsetting them? How do they implement a combative philosophy without pushing a client to the exits?

Enter Gregory Diehl, an up-and-coming life coach who's written three books and consulted with internet start-ups. He hosts a popular travel podcast. He's marketed as a travel consultant, having lived in fifty countries in the last twelve years. He has taught in locations like rural China, Iraq, Ecuador, and Armenia. He's written a book on the matter called *Travel as Transformation*, which he self-published. His books produce a reliable income stream.

Diehl claims his primary technique in life coaching is a strategy he coined: strategic aggravation, he calls it. He works to upset the ebb and flow of coach-client communication, with persistent questions and skepticism. He is dismissive, argumentative, and at times downright rude.

At thirty, he is already a kind of guru life coach, with a loyal following of readers of his books and listeners to his podcasts. He comes recommended by an actor friend who considers Diehl the toughest life coach in the world. "He doesn't care what you think coming in," the actor says. "I don't even think he cares what you end up thinking. He wants to see your thinking and rethinking as it happens. He's impatient and demanding. But it works somehow. He makes you stronger."

As with many life coaches, Diehl's connection to this client occurred through word of mouth. The actor likes Diehl's writing, is a loyal listener to Diehl's podcasts, and reads his books. He learned of Diehl from a personal trainer who, while traveling in Malaysia, heard him mentioned in a podcast on travel. "He'll scare you," the trainer said. "He wants you to be in pain. He's kind of a grumpy guy," he said. "He scolds. And doesn't encourage you, really. He's like an old-time football coach. He's just sort of over you from the get-go. Kind of an asshole, I guess. He's just tough."

"I'm not tough," Diehl later says via Skype, shaking his head. "I simply believe you can only make discoveries through difficult experiences, and most people avoid difficult experiences as much as they can."

The difficult experience he has in mind is travel, of course, which most people associate with relaxation. Diehl sees the value of discomfort in travel. For him, the danger comes in seeking out the same sorts of comforts again and again. "If you've only lived within a narrow range of experiences," he says, "and they are repeating throughout your life, you have a limited understanding of what you like and what you don't like, what you value and you don't value. I challenge that in my sessions."

The Skype connection wavers. He offers to connect again in an hour. He's in the Philippines tonight, on an island. "I'm in a city now," he says. The thought of it seems to make him sigh in resignation. "I do not care for cities." Then he disconnects.

DIEHL LEFT SAN DIEGO at eighteen, weeks after his high school graduation. He was living in a van, playing guitar and selling drugs to get by. He'd been thrown out of high school several times. "One of the times I wasn't wearing shoes and another time I was selling drugs out of my van that I lived in. I got the diploma and never once have I ever needed a high school diploma in my entire adult life," he says. It seems he's told this story too many times to count, and feels as if he knows that no one will get it in the end.

He made a living traveling abroad by teaching English,

mixed in with a measure of manual labor, moving around Central America and China. Despite his disparaging remarks about public education, he became a kind of intellectual. He spent the years after high school reading a lot. Apparently, he read a lot while he was in high school as well. Asked when he became a reader, Diehl doesn't have to look into himself very deeply. He seems to think that the self he became is the self he always was—the same at ten that he was at eighteen. Same as the one he is today. He's completely sure of the truth of this. "At ten years old, I became hyper-aware of myself and the world I was living in. I was reading then. I felt then, as a child and later as a teenager, very stifled by the authority figures in my life, which included my parents, school, pretty much everyone. And I was reading then too."

Most life coaches are reticent about revealing their own lives. Diehl is a different animal. You must know his story in order to understand his perspective. He dishes it out bit by bit, sounding oppositional and clichéd at the same time. There are always drug dealers without shoes living in a van somewhere; there are always kids flying overseas with not enough money in their pockets. But you don't normally expect them to end up as wise people, sought out by others, and paid by them, in order to gain clarity.

After he ditched the van he went to Costa Rica. He flew. He didn't have his parents' blessing. He's pretty sure of that anyway. He doesn't seem to have tried to verify the statement in the twelve years since. "I'm certain they had many things to think and to say about my move," he says, "but none that was relevant to my decision making." Whoa.

He seems a smidgen bored, dragging himself through this familiar storytelling territory. From the other end—as interviewer—I sense the right coaching move for the present moment is to interrupt the familiar routine and create a new direction. "Why would you go off to a foreign country without the money to get back? What were you after? Wouldn't the most practical way have been to suck it up and save your money first?"

"No, because I wouldn't have had the independence then. It was the most cost-effective way to be independent."

What would a life coach have told you? I ask.

"I don't use life coaches," he states flatly.

A life coach who doesn't use life coaches. Fair enough. "But what would you tell an eighteen-year-old who's been selling drugs and all the rest, when he wanted to move to Costa Rica with not enough money? Be a life coach for a minute."

"If everything was a precursor to travel?" he says. "I

would just say: Go." And so he sends his past self into the unknown, which is not unknown at all at this point.

Let's reset. Gregory Diehl is a life coach. You can never really be sure where he's living. He has homes in Ecuador and Armenia. So you might start at his website (https://www.gregorydiehl.net/coaching/). He lists no credentials or certifications. He doesn't have any. But he is admirably frank in terms of his goals and outcomes for clients.

The site opens with a statement outlining the nuts and bolts of the program, which lasts three months, and stating the kind of commitment Diehl wants from clients. There's a bullet-pointed list in which Diehl asserts that he will help clients:

- Evolve recurring thought patterns and emotions
- Discover core values
- Form meaningful relationships
- Peacefully dissolve harmful social ties
- Understand the real motivations behind actions
- Achieve psychological freedom

You can't really lose with any of this. Forming meaning-ful relationships seems sensible enough, while dissolving harmful social ties feels vague, if laudable.

The site's second list sounds a bit more like a series of promises. "After working with me," it reads, the client will:

- Have clarity on who you are and what you want in life
- Align your intellect with your emotions
- Pursue important goals with purpose
- Communicate intimately and authentically
- Live with confidence in the knowledge of who you are
- Approach obstacles with pride and strategy

It is a broad list. Diehl says he models these outcomes on his own development. This produces a short pause in the conversation. "That's confidence," he says. "I ask my clients to make a radical transformation." Another silence, then he expertly turns the tables. Life coach.

"Do you think I'm arrogant?" he asks. There's an answer given, but does it matter? Diehl is preternaturally calm, but he does seem vaguely annoyed. "I just have very clear standards of human behavior for myself and for others. I try to embody those standards. I create arguments about behavior with my clients. They have to pick their words carefully when confronting me because I'm getting them to their core beliefs. As for the list, I'm confident of my ability to lead people to these points of transformation."

LIKE MOST LIFE COACHES, Diehl keeps a small roster of active clients, whom he generally meets with once a week. He begins the relationship by providing a complimentary session to anyone applying through the website; this allows him to evaluate his and the prospective client's fit. He rejects clients fairly often. Diehl admits that he does this for his own reasons: he needs to avoid boredom. "Part of why I started writing books was because I didn't want to keep having the same conversations over and over anymore. People kept asking me the same questions, and I had to keep telling the same stories, explaining the same things. I figured: I'll just put those in a book, and then people can just read that book and not have to keep talking to me personally."

Why even offer life coaching if you're so put out by such questions? Why work to motivate others when you're trying so hard to become less accessible and forthcoming yourself?

It's not for the money, he says. People buy his books, which now produce enough passive income for him to live on. Life coaching sometimes gets taxing and repetitive. "I've been constantly redefining the kind of work I want to be doing personally with people. I don't want to get stuck in the loop that many life coaches do."

In his podcasts, Diehl has often stated his belief that life coaching is "bullshit." He's asserted—to his listeners, who might reasonably be considered potential life-coaching clients—that typical life coaches develop formulas and scripts that they follow. "They just keep asking the same questions, offering the same generic guidance. Everybody's just running in place the whole time. It works well for the coaches because they keep a full roster of clients and they keep getting paid. But it's the same thing, over and over again."

Again, I feel the need to shift gears, to interrupt the routine, so I ask: How much do you change for your sessions? But Diehl mishears my voice through a rumble on the internet and thinks I've said "charge" not "change."

He remains unfazed. "I don't ever want to turn anyone down for financial reasons, especially if I truly think that it's a good fit for them to work with me," he says. At the same time, he says, he likes to keep a high dollar value on his time because he assumes the client will get more out of the coaching if they're investing a lot in it.

He demurs on the price point for a moment, perhaps fearing to induce a kind of sticker shock. He usually employs weekly phone meetings, which may run an hour, two, or even longer. He and the client work until whatever it is they are talking about has been resolved. "And the cost may be as little as a few hundred dollars a month," he says, "if that's what I think they can afford. Other times it could be two or three thousand a month. I have to judge."

When I returned to the original question—how much do you change your sessions from one to the next?—he clears his throat. "None of my sessions are the same," he says. "All human interactions differ. I don't repeat myself, and when I do it's a sign that I'm bored."

So what?

He looks up, to his left. "So, I remove myself," he says.

Diehl claims it is not difficult to maintain his client base. "I do not pursue clients," he says. "They pursue me." Age is sometimes an issue with a new client. Typically, the ones who come his way are his age or younger. (Most life coaches report a similar occurrence, including Pervis Taylor, who is in his late thirties, and Markita Collins, who is thirty-four.) There is, all of them believe, the presumption of a sort of wisdom gap that makes older clients less likely to select a younger life coach. "Most older people don't like taking advice from someone younger than themselves," Diehl says. He writes this off easily enough. "It's a social signaling thing. They want to feel like the more experienced, worldly one."

Most of his clients are men. Many work in internet start-ups or speculative ventures. "I think I appeal more to men than women," he says, "and I definitely interact with most women differently than [I do with] men, because I think women are looking for something different than what I offer. Most women aren't as inclined to being yelled at, for example. Just speaking stereotypically, of course."

Hold up. Yelled at? Are you yelling at people?

He admits that he is. It is one of his tools of confrontation. "Sometimes a man needs to feel it. So I'll yell: *What the fuck are you doing with your life?*"

Not a bad question in and of itself. One that each of us probably asks ourselves now and again. But why yell? Is there a particular value in startling someone? Is loudness a kind of tool? Life coaches seek to create some measure of interruption in their clients' existing patterns of behavior. Most do it by means of inquiry alone, trusting that reflection on a carefully worded question will lead to realizations.

A threatening trigger like yelling would seem to inhibit such a thoughtful response. Diehl feels otherwise. "I just want their first response," he says, "as quickly as possible, before their mind gets in the way."

"Sometimes a client needs a little emotional kick in the ass. Raising your voice or cursing can be the way to do that," he says, "if it's done tastefully and effectively." In psychology, this sort of provocation is sometimes used in "rage therapy" with trauma victims, challenging them to unmask their repressed anger and yell back at their therapist. Yelling leads to a clarification of emotions, and can help begin a process of healing. So it seems like a practical form of strategic aggravation, though why it's useful for men but not for women remains obscure.

"Well, I wouldn't want you to think it's the only way I interact with people," Diehl says. He simply feels that raising his voice, confronting his clients with their own contradictions, puts the onus on them to redefine their thinking.

Diehl stumbles into a box canyon of troublesome gender stereotypes when speaking of his relationship with female clients. "I think I appeal more to people with masculine personalities than feminine ones," he says. When pushed, he cites his frankness, a quality he seems to associate mostly with men. "My approach is very direct. It's stern, no beating around the bush." Men take to that, he says, women less so.

He claims to have met exceptions to his rule. "I've met women who don't seem to think much like typical young women. They seem very intelligent. They seem very directed, very straightforward, and they often have trouble identifying with other young women because they seem to think more like men. They appreciate me more for that reason."

In moments like these, Diehl seems as out of touch with the times we live in as he is far removed from his contemporaries in physical distance. He sounds a bit like a character in a Graham Greene novel, sitting in a bar in a remote corner of the tropics, holding forth on women he hasn't seen in more than a decade. Either that, or he is purposely working to incite an argument. It feels like a moment of strategic aggravation. The response percolates in my head. I don't believe there is a masculine personality. Or a feminine one. Why is he so willing to measure women's intelligence based on their response to him? He's staring into the Skype app now, smiling at me. Wait. Did we just stumble into this impasse, or has he been trying to get the listener to pick a fight? At that point I remember what he said early on: The client has to learn to pick their words for the first time in confronting him. They need to revisit core beliefs. Argument too can be a form of personal growth. And so I resist. I don't like traps. He laughs a little before we move on.

DIEHL ONLY SPENDS A few hours a week at the computer, and he's still in the process of determining who his ideal client is. "Again," he says, "I really don't want to work with the wrong kind of people."

"And the wrong kind of people would be . . . ?" I interject. "People who just aren't open to your ideas? Or . . . I think you've touched on this elsewhere, but maybe you can tell me a little bit. The wrong person would be someone who what?"

Diehl narrows his gaze, looks deep into the lens of his computer's camera. "The wrong person would be somebody who's looking for a very general conception of personal development and people that *are* life coaches.

"Life coaches, uh-huh," I note. "A narrow conception? Or a general one? Which did you say?"

"General," he replies.

"Okay. A very loose conception of personal development," I repeat. "Got it."

"I don't want to work with a client who just wants to be told what they already want to hear. I'm really much more the opposite. I'm much more likely to give the negative feedback than the positive feedback.

"Positive feedback won't work for them," he says. "I'm more likely to begin by trying to understand how someone thinks, their paradigm, their desires, why they want what they want, and look for *inconsistencies* in those things. Or the incompleteness of those things.

"People think they want something when they come to me," he says. "But they don't know why they want it, where that desire came from, or why they think something works a certain way. I'd ask, 'Well, why do you think that? I'm not saying you're wrong, necessarily, I just want to know why you think that's true. Do you know why you think it's true?'"

More often than not, he says, clients won't have a good idea how to answer those sorts of questions. They are rife with internal contradictions, he says. "And if there are contradictions, clearly at least one of those things must be wrong, and contradictions cannot stand, and very often, everything else is wrong because they've never actually given serious thought to these kinds of important questions.

"I get bored really easily," he says. "I'm always looking for something new to learn, some new uncomfortably challenging experience to immerse myself in. It makes me particularly good at making other people uncomfortable too, this fact that I like to make myself uncomfortable in learning."

These are the essential underpinnings of his book *Travel as Transformation*: short, strangely surreal in its conception, a travelogue tracing his journey from San Diego to Manchuria and back. It's got a small wolflike following on the internet. The message is simple enough: traveling to difficult places can have a profound effect on your understanding of the world by undermining your assumptions about yourself. The book is a reflection of Diehl's methods as a life coach.

DUSTIN JACKSON IS A staff software engineer at a software development firm in Silicon Valley, who agreed to speak about his sessions with Diehl provided I change his name. He met Diehl after reading his book *Travel as Trans-*

formation three years ago. He looked Diehl up on Facebook, and the two developed a long-term client-coach relationship. "I loved the book, and talking to him was incredibly refreshing. Conversations in my life can be quite dry and superficial."

Jackson says he never heard Diehl mention strategic aggravation, but claims it makes sense that he would use that term. "He's not one of the hyper-empathic, hyper-feeling, trauma-healing, focused-listening-but-not-real-opinions kind of coaches. He startles me. He can be adversarial, provocative during our coaching, but that's not his only coaching technique. I'd say that style of communication accounts for ten to twenty percent of our time." Asked for a concrete example of how Diehl helped, Jackson cites a session in which he spoke of how he had put off filing his taxes until it was too late. By the time of the session, he was feeling that the IRS was minutes away from knocking on his door. He was convinced he had screwed up his life irreparably. Diehl responded to this anxiety by making fun of him. "He did a sort of parody of how I articulated my problem to him, pretty funny too, mirroring me back to myself in a cartoonish way. That snapped me out of believing my own narrative. All of a sudden I saw myself as this character, caught in a state of panic. I reacted to the character instead of my fear. Eventually with his help, I got my taxes filed, and a massive anxiety was lifted off my shoulders."

Jackson is clear on the principles Diehl emphasizes. "Self-reliance, independent, rational thought," he says. "He only pushes your buttons when you're not logical, or he pushes them when you settle for mediocrity." Does he make you feel uncomfortable? Does he yell at you? Jackson is asked, via e-mail. He demurs slightly. "He'll try to jar you when you're stuck in a story, or are sitting unaware of the rest of the world."

Jackson seems legitimately grateful for the work he's done with Diehl. "I've been very lonely at times," he says. "I don't really connect with people who seem to embrace life without really questioning the most basic suppositions given to them by family, culture, religion, country. I like the questioning Gregory does. Just having a friend who's dissected even the most rudimentary of things about being a human has really helped me feel less lonely, and allowed me to relax more into the own odd/alien path that I carve through life."

DIEHL WORKS TO GET his clients to understand the patterns of their bad habits. Why do you care about these things? he asks. Then asks again. Why does this problem cause you so much distress? What brought you to this point? He then turns them toward solutions. "The solution may be completely different than what was expected. It may involve a sacrifice, or the deconstruction of elements of themselves that they weren't necessarily prepared to give up when they came into the sessions. They may have to tell a secret. Who knows?" he says. "I have to poke certain uncomfortable pressure points. A lot. And often. [The client] may even shout at me before it's over."

Asked if he ever just calls the client on their bullshit, Diehl bristles. "Most of the time I'm just working with the information the client gives me. That's why, when reviewing with a client, I usually look for internal contradictions, like, 'Earlier you said this, and now you're saying this. Those two things really don't go together.'"

"I don't *start* arguments anyway," he corrects himself. "It only becomes an argument," he says, "if there's repeated conflict between me and a client."

In many ways, Diehl engages in the most elemental sort of life-coaching technique of them all. He listens like hell and repeats what he's been told as a question. But he differs from the others in that he's very willing to make connections for the client, in order to accelerate the process. He presents hypotheses that allow clients to push back. He presents options. Does he give advice?

"I don't give advice," he says. "Because I don't care enough to."

So it is fair to say that you seek out disagreement? That you create conflict? Clients do that for him, Diehl says. "Most people don't know where their presumptions come from," he says. "They don't really understand their core beliefs." Clients behave very calmly when talking about the truths they bank on in life. But Diehl feels that speaking slowly and calmly doesn't indicate any particular certainty. "It often indicates fear," he says. "So I tend to jump on that pretty quickly." Sometimes his clients need to be coaxed into a deeper reaction; sometimes he has to prod them to shoot back an answer in anger.

"Quite often they'll just keep restating their disagreement," he says, "which never gets them anywhere near the answer." The client is just resisting change in those moments. Flexing the muscles of practiced rhetoric. "So I have to keep countering that by saying, 'Why are you saying that? Where does that come from? Why do you think that's untrue? You haven't answered the question.'" Now he's asking the questions a life coach would ask. Seemingly benign. Unthreatening. Smallish. Urgings to examine the way conclusions were reached rather than the conclusions themselves.

The conversation continues. "So what was the original question here?" I ask.

Diehl smiles. Guru. "Money," he says. "That's where we started. What do I value about money?"

But what wasn't it at all. The money question was one that he proposed, probably a question *he* wanted to answer. "That wasn't it," I say, checking my notes.

But Diehl seems unable to let that stand. "Okay," he says, sounding a little miffed. "What do *you* value so much about money?"

Before I undertake an answer, I sigh. "You're exhausting," I assert, which doesn't make him laugh. Clearly, he's been working me over. "Do clients ever end up hating you?" I say.

Diehl doesn't seem to consider the implications of my asking this question. He answers directly. "They don't hate me at first," he says. "But, come on, if they're the kind of person who's going to end up hating me because of something trivial, they probably shouldn't be working with me in the first place."

That's the first thing he's said that isn't easy to argue with, which is probably just the way Gregory Diehl likes it.

5

NOT A PSYCHOLOGIST

Markita Collins, 34
South Mountain, PA

She whips through her life. Her church, her house, her children, her writing, her business, her husband's business, her children again, then her house, then a long evening of phone sessions with her roster of thirty clients, most of them women, most Christian, many on their way to becoming life coaches themselves, who live in three North American time zones, and others in Europe and Africa. Tomorrow she'll travel to Dallas to lead a seminar. Then back for church Sunday night.

Markita Collins is a whirlwind. She centers all this out of an office on the second floor of her house in South Mountain, Pennsylvania, a little dot on the map between Philadelphia and Pittsburgh. Her husband, a graphic designer, shares the space when he's home. She's marketing her writing. Her four children rule the rest of the house, as children will, when they are not sleeping. She calls me, at 11:43 p.m. Eastern Standard Time, with an hour or two to talk, before she goes back to work . . . before she finally goes to sleep.

Even this late, Collins appears impossibly collected. Smiling. Joking. Radiant. She's quick to tell you she's a mother, a minister, a motivational speaker, a vocalist, and most of all, a certified life coach. In her life as a coach, she works mostly with women of color. Women of color who want to be stronger mothers, live as better Christians, and become successful entrepreneurs. "I wear a lot of hats," Collins says. "And I mean that literally, you know? Really. I mean, I go to church pretty regular. A lot of hats in life. But I wear a lot of coaching hats in the work I do."

Collins's clients don't draw a line between their need for spiritual counsel and their desire for a career in life coaching. Collins will be the first to say, "My life coaching has a purpose." She declares, "I come to it from the world of preaching and ministering to my people." She is careful to explain that she is a trained, certified life coach. Her clients pay her. Collins uses the tools of life coaching as a means of providing the tools of change.

"In a lot of ways, I know I just love people back to life," she says. "That keeps them on a path. It changes their perception about what this whole world is when they feel the love, even from the life coach. And I don't provoke my clients . . . I don't pick at them. If they don't feel beaten into changing, they can be loved into it." She seems to speak without pauses, even this late at night. "So you see, I'm not just a motivational speaker, a minister of the church, or a regular life coach. Or a mother. I'm all of that."

LIKE ANY GOOD LIFE coach, she places the work of change in the lap of the client. She speaks of giving them tools. She asks questions. "About their mind-sets," she says. "The way they've survived so far has not been enough." She provides them with exercises. Decisions are the province of the client, but Collins makes her faith an important part of her sessions. "I'm not afraid to ask if I might pray with them," she says. "That's often a rhythm we both know. Some clients ask for that. But I have many clients who don't want prayer. They learn very early on that's perfectly fine. They see me as someone who helps them think about marketing their own ideas, their own services." She acknowledges this apparent divide in her nationally attended spiritual seminars on women and faith. "Marketing helps spread the word," she says. "Messaging is a tool of faith. Those terms might sound funny, but it's always been that way."

So, call her a spiritual life coach. But don't disregard the aspect of entrepreneurial coaching inspired by her business and branding acumen. That's how she lays it out. And she coaches young mothers too. "I like to say I mother them," she says. "I've been a mother for my entire adult life. I know you can feel alone at it, and—say you don't have your own family to lean on—it's hard to know how to ask for help."

The majority of her clients are African American women, between twenty-five and forty-five. Collins doesn't mind admitting that she feels her work fills a need in the African American community. "In our community, we've been told we don't need therapists. We've been told—we've told each other, 'Just be strong. Just pray. You're too strong to need therapy.'

"We've looked down on therapy. Period. And whether you are a woman or a man, as an African American, you have been taught that you don't need it." Collins heard this opinion in her roles as a woman and as a minister. She saw that it was harmful to cut off lines of support—like therapy—to people in need. "I totally reject the idea that black women don't need therapy. There's no wisdom in cutting ourselves off to ideas, to help. That's not what the Bible teaches. It's just foolish to live in this world, with things in your brain that you can't break down because you are prevented access to the tools to do it. We can't internalize everything. We make ourselves crazy doing that."

Collins navigates the space between the two jobs—ministering and life coaching—in all aspects of her work. She connects them more often than most life coaches will suggest is possible, and she works to do that without co-opting the mission of either job. "As a minister, I'll be working with a client and we'll be working to pray our way through some questions. Or I'll present the person with some questions designed to help find change in reflection on themelves. But sometimes I just say no, you need to go sit on a psychologist's couch to get some answers. And I'm not a psychologist. I don't treat people. I help them train themselves. But I'm not afraid to say, 'Let's take this a step further and get you some help.'"

But how does a coach use her own life of faith in the development of a loyal client base, both paying and nonpaying? Does her strong faith allow Collins to blur the line between Christian and non-Christian? Isn't it possible that the evangelical style leans toward proselytizing over personal change?

"What I learned through my coaching training is the importance of not forcing your ideas on other people," she says. "They teach you. You don't give them the answer. You help them navigate. That's what the best ministers do too."

Collins was raised in the church from birth. Her family and community reinforced her connection to it. So why did she start life-coach training at all? When her children started going to school, Collins felt she had something to offer other women whose situations resembled hers. As mother, aspiring businesswoman, leader in church. A lot of hats.

It was then that she started entertaining an idea for a book. Outlining that book helped her feel like she could bridge the gaps between her several worlds. With faith in the notion that she could excel in many things, without betraying her values, she put the book aside and made her life even more complicated by becoming a life coach.

She felt that she needed new tools in order to be able to teach others. Having spent little time in college, she did not consider herself much of a student. And there was no time.

Already in her late twenties, she did not feel that she had eight to ten years to pursue the degree necessary to practice as a therapist.

For a year and a half she trained online, and at home, to get credentialed as a life coach. "My certification is in Neuro Linguistic Programming. They teach life coaching, they use the hypnosis. I'm not much on the hypnosis. I don't practice that. But I got my certification through a mixture of learning modules, online training, and hands-on training. I wanted the most serious training I could get when I started."

She completed the accreditation process through the International Coach Federation online, where she was allowed to work at her own pace through twelve learning modules set up by ICF in their program offices in England. "It took me about six months to do it," she says. "I chose the course work because it felt as intense as the responsibility of coaching did. And I didn't want to stall."

She realizes that she might have hung a shingle and called herself a coach without any course work at all, just using her experience to date. "I wanted something real," she says. "I wanted techniques I understood fully. Not a wham-bang three-day seminar in a hotel somewhere, and you-can-coach kind of thing. Sometimes it was tough, because I wanted to get to work. And, yes, I even wanted to earn money." She finished the program believing that life-coach training could allow her to strengthen her work as a minister, not weaken it.

The course work let her know that there was more to life coaching than intuition. She just wanted the information, and a means to get at the knowledge and techniques. She needed to know how others did life coaching before she could decide how she would practice it herself.

"I really didn't want to invent a system of coaching; I wanted to rely on one. It wasn't a matter of 'Oh, I have this gift' or 'I have this passion to be a life coach.' I wanted a framework, and I needed that framework to do my work.

SAMANTHA PITTS, A THIRTY-SEVEN-YEAR-OLD financial staff member at a Fortune 500 company and one of Collins's life-coach clients, particularly values Collins's candid acknowledgment and inclusion of her roots in the church. She came across Collins's work at an entrepreneurial conference in Georgia two summers before meeting with her. "At a spiritual conference like that, most people are uncomfortable with working to sell the work that they've done, or why you should make the investment, or purchase their product. Ms. Markita wasn't like that at all. She basically said, 'This is my book. You should have it in your life.' Her husband was there at the table too. That stood out to me. So direct. So confident. She was very approachable."

She picked up on Collins's social media feeds immediately, and in the days after the conference, she was able to deepen her understanding of who Collins was. "I would watch her casually on Periscope, and I liked how funny and real she was." It was not the religious connection that struck Pitts so much as Collins's sense of humor. "She's not super churchy or off-putting. She is really kind of like the girlfriend you can have a talk with. The aunty or the sister. She's very fluid in the hats, the various hats that she wears."

Soon after the conference, Pitts started in with the one-on-one sessions. She emphasizes the comfort she derives from the fixed structure of the sessions. "There are rituals. Open up with prayer. She might record the prayer and send it to me. I like that. You talk about what's on your heart. She's someone I'm talking about ideas with, like doing life together, and we get better at it. From there, I would say there's a recap, and then homework usually follows after that. We close with something that leads back to solidifying our relationship and identity with God. But it's a very free-flowing conversation, so it doesn't feel like church. But it also doesn't feel like I'm sitting on a couch talking to a psychiatrist."

FIVE YEARS LATER, COLLINS is deep in it. She's a speaker at national seminars on spirituality and self-improvement, a preacher at her church, and an author. She carries a full slate of clients in her subscription-based life-coaching business, which has three levels of access, two of which pay her, through her website. "I have about thirty regular clients that I work with monthly," she says. "I work with them in sessions, at night. Sometimes it might be thirty minutes, sometimes it can go to an hour. For me, it might run from four calls to six calls a day.

"And then I have this other layer of service, what I call Kita's Kompany, which I run through my website. It's a subscription-level service for people who just want to get a feel for me. It involves chat groups, pop-up classes, Q-and-As. I come on social media and I coach them through a group chat as opposed to just the one-on-one. Other times,

I do life coaching and some encouragement ministering to people on Periscope."

Collins makes no bones about the fact that she learned the basics of life coaching from various people in her church life. "I had great teachers, great guides throughout my life in the church." Catering to Christians and non-Christians alike broadens her potential client base.

"People have boundaries. I understand that. I can still help anybody; I just let them know up front: this is who I am. So I'm giving them that much right away. Usually, even if it's someone who is not a Christian, or someone who doesn't believe the faith that I walk in, they're still open because I have trained as a coach, and have a record as one."

Has Collins spread herself a bit too thin between her extensive use of social media and the demands of her life in the church? "I fight with that," she says. "The urge to give everything to whoever needs it next. I had to protect myself. My life-coaching schedule, and the income it produces, help me to structure that demand."

Her business is growing as she gets more proficient in dealing with a larger and larger client base. "Some people do a one-and-done. They just call once, then quit. Some of them never come back. But most clients say: I gotta come back. I need this. It's worth it. As a life coach, you learn to value yourself and you put a price on your energy. I can't be around time wasters. My time is too valuable."

ASKED TO DESCRIBE THE changes she sees in the women she works with, Collins hesitates just long enough to make a choice from her list. "Two years ago, I met an individual dealing with some severe low self-esteem." This woman, who worked as a phlebotomist in a maternity clinic, had a strong if vague sense that she was supposed to be doing something more, but she could not see what it was. She felt defeated by her situation, saw her self-worth only in terms of her job, which had begun to feel disconnected with the mission of the clinic. Her colleagues delivered babies. She merely drew blood. Should she change jobs? Should she move? She felt she did not have the courage to make even minimal changes. She came to Collins barely able to voice her certainty that it was time for her to step out and do something about her life. She just couldn't find the strength.

The phlebotomist found Collins through a link sent by her church. She e-mailed Collins and asked for a one-on-

one meeting, without being able to describe what exactly she wanted, except change.

Rather than asking for a great deal of background information, or attempting to trace the origin of the woman's low self-esteem, Collins simply asked the phlebotomist to name her capabilities. Create a list of them. This kind of inventorying is a classic life-coach starting point, putting the client in the now, leaning toward the future. "Mothering," the phlebotomist said right off the bat.

Collins was intrigued. To her knowledge, the woman had no children, and was not in a relationship with anyone who did. She had not mentioned any children in her life or listed being a mother as one of her jobs. But Collins let the phlebotomist continue without questioning. "Your biggest job as a life coach is to listen. And I like to talk, but I let her do the telling. I just waited. And then she said, 'Even though I'm not a biological mom, I'm still a mom.'" Collins asked: Of whom? And the phlebotomist answered: "I'm a mom of many."

Collins raises her eyebrows in the telling of this story. "Now, I like to assign people their own slogans," she says. "I said right then: that's your slogan. We returned to that again and again." The phlebotomist had helped other women raise their children through many jobs in her life, even with the blood draws she did in her current work. She believed her connection to children made her stronger as a person. She saw herself as a kind of mother, but she felt unseen in this capacity.

It took more than one session, but her progress was steady. "First, I had to get her to admit that she had a fear of people rejecting her because she was not a biological mother. I had to help her get past her fear of rational people saying: How can you be a mom of many, when you don't have any children of your own? So we spent some time working to filter through that so she could say: Hey, I may not have natural children, but I've raised many children."

And is the world supposed to believe that this was a result of doing blood draws for a living?

Collins frowns at the question. "It came more from taking care of siblings, taking care of her neighbors' children, babysitting, doing day care, and serving in her church ministry, where she would go to the day care and perform nanny services. She had worked with a lot of musical artists, and when those artists went out of town, she would tend to their children. She pretty much raised some of those children. That's what she fell into as a young woman. It's what she knew. But she didn't understand that she could turn that into a business."

Collins helped her figure this out by reinforcing the phlebotomist's self-image. "I told her you may not have birth children, but you're very much a mother. You're nurturing, you're caring, you're loving. You're not just letting children grow up before your eyes, you're training them up, you're raising them, you're cultivating them." The phlebotomist didn't want to work with children, however. She wanted to have a wider impact. She wanted to use her many mothering experiences to connect to other mothers.

Collins helped her get started thinking about a means to connect to larger groups of mothers. "She ended up turning that into a business, and she's doing very well with that now. I offered to teach her some coaching skills. I pointed her to the training. We crafted questions for young mothers. Now she does a coaching program for moms, helping moms unpack the tremendous responsibilities they take on with children."

The phlebotomist took Collins's work and passed it on. "That's the best thing about coaching for me . . . to see people go beyond where they thought they were going to go, the moments when they exceed their own expectations . . . to see the people follow through and not give up. That's best for me when it goes beyond the simple transformation, when it starts to be about the following through. Maybe that's God's work. Everything is God's work. But *they* did it. They come to me having the potential to finish, but they can't. I get to see people follow through, to work with them to get it done, not for me, but for themselves . . . that is amazing. That is a joy for me."

This past year, Collins finished the book that traces her path and her career, titled *I'm Still Old Fashioned*, a self-published memoir that connects Collins's self-professed old-school family values with her drive to be a modern entrepreneur, a teacher, and survivor. She believes every life coach has a book inside them. The book was a milestone for Collins, but there have been other key moments as well. "Writing a book has been a key component in the acquisition of clients," she says. "You need to write a book. It translates you to your potential client base in advance of your work. It's an income stream. It tells who you are . . . My book tells my story, so I don't have to [tell it] in coaching sessions. I don't talk about myself there. The book talks for me. It makes me relatable; let's people see my triumphs, my victories, my downfalls. It shows how I had to press through a lot of adversity through relationships, childhood, bullying, abuse, and all of that mental anguish, depression, and how I was able to get through all of these things using certain principles that I've applied to my everyday life."

As for the everyday life of life coach Markita Collins, it should be known that she works with a larger number of clients than any of the life coaches featured in this book. She leads online group classes, increasing her client base, and travels around the country appearing at seminars and conferences. She's a charismatic, energetic, funny, and magnetic presence. Women sit through her seminar sessions and then line up in conference center hallways to meet her. Given the demands on her time and energy, it's amazing that she still is able to have memorable one-on-one relationships with her clients.

LIKE MANY LIFE COACHES in these times, Collins rarely sees her one-on-one clients in the flesh, as they are spread out across the country. She laundry-lists their locations. "I have clients in California, in Chicago. I have clients in Ohio, Florida, and Texas. I have two clients in Arizona, and others in Pennsylvania. I have clients in London." Then she adds, "I also have clients in Africa."

These one-on-one clients typically pay $350 per session. "Not by the hour," she clarifies: by the session. "Eventually, if they decide to work with me monthly, and they make a commitment to that, they get a discount. But $350 is where it starts."

It seems a decent living, in South Mountain, Pennsylvania. Collins smiles. "I am making a living. I really am. At first it was hard for me to charge people, because I am a minister. That's where it gets funny, right? I'm an ordained minister, and I'm a relationship strategist. And it got real funny, because I'd start to feel like I shouldn't be charging people because I'm a Christian. But I always remind myself, this is my vocation. I studied for this. I worked for this, so yeah. It's a very decent living."

She laughs, more a thank-my-lucky-stars kind of thing than a cackle. She squints straight into the camera lens on her computer. "When I started, my time used to run fifty dollars a session. I would be on the phone for hours, and make only fifty dollars. I was like: 'Wake up, girl. You're doing a lot.'" And she smiles, a bit triumphant and a bit conspiratorial, speaking on Skype, late at night. "So yeah. $350 an hour. That's what it is. And I know that that's gonna increase eventually.

But she notes that she is in the habit of surprising her clients with a phone call out of the blue. When reminded of this, she calls out loud: "Absolutely!" She calls these pop-up calls. "That's a tool I use. I just randomly call to say: 'Hey, how are you doing? What's going on? How are you feeling today? I thought about you.' That's the most human kind of connection. Inquiring. I'm just modeling a kind of connection. And I don't want anything from them. I tell them it's not an exercise. I just want you to check in; they do some kind of assessment in those moments. They get mindful. And they love that.

"And pop-up calls are free," she adds brightly.

Most of her clients are women; most are serious Christians. But Collins does not see that as limiting. "I'm a woman, and so initially it's reasonable that I attract other women to my practice. But I'm open to helping men as well. I'm not closed off; men need healing too. I feel like I'm down with the heart, I'm down with love, I'm down with making sure everybody is good.

"I literally help people heal while they build, whether it's building a business, building relationships, building their confidence, building their brand, building their self-worth. I help people heal in areas that other people won't touch, and I'm not afraid to go into those places so they can face it so they can move forward. So that's really my power. That works for men just as well as women."

Her goal for clients as a life coach is far different than that of a minister. It separates the work for her. "A minister wants people to walk a path. It's a path they've studied. The triumph is to recognize and walk that path that faith provides. A path they walk themselves," she says. "As a life coach, I most want people to *find* their path. No matter what that path is. It works with me because as I said, it's the love that draws people. I'm not forcing what I believe on them. I'm a life coach. I'm letting you be open and we're just gonna have this honest conversation, and we're going to figure out what's really going on."

And looking back, what's your advice to a person just setting out in the field? Can you speak to a woman who feels she hasn't received the picture-perfect college preparation for life coaching? Can such women join the field of life coaching with something to offer?

"That's easy," she says. "Definitely do your research. Everything that's offered on the internet is not for you. Look for substance. Always check the receipts."

Most of all, have confidence in yourself as a life coach,

she says. "People want to know that you can help them solve their problems. So solve your own. They don't care *who* you know. They want to sense that you can help them, to know that you have helped others. So do the work yourself. Get a life coach. Find your own answers and pay attention to how you did it. And when you know you're a problem solver, do your research. If you get the right information, you can do this. You can definitely do this. That's what I would tell them."

JUST A LIFE COACH. MAYBE.

So where does that leave us? Five coaches, each with a different expertise, training, professional experience, social media skills, and attitude toward their mission and their clients. Hearing their words reveals some of the diversity of background and approach that defines the life-coaching trade. There is no such thing as a model life coach, though there are many models to follow.

We might all agree that the world of life coaching is a bit like the Wild West. There's a hell of a lot of frontier, for one thing. The future is bright. New life coaches set out for that frontier all the time. And there isn't much in the way of law out there. Certified coaches, and the institutions that trained them, might wear the badge, but there are a lot of free-ranging life coaches on the frontier, using their wit, wisdom, and expertise, representing civilization very nicely. Badge or no badge, there is no sheriff; no single life coach is in charge.

How do you know if you possess the talent to become a life coach? What are the requirements you need to fulfill in order to advocate for another person selflessly? Who do you turn to to help you obtain the techniques, exercises, and associated materials that will allow you to develop your own program—a program that will get you through more than a couple of crackling conversations with a paying client? How do you lead a person to change without jamming their nose into the door? What should you want for them? And for yourself?

You might work down this checklist.

Are you interested in other people?	Yes/No
Are you able to resist judgment of others?	Yes/No
Do you possess the ability to follow up?	Yes/No
Can you keep a secret (without a professional bond)?	Yes/No
Are you empathetic?	Yes/No
Are you curious?	Yes/No
Are you interested in building a business?	Yes/No

ANSWERING NO TO ANY one of these items has absolutely no bearing on your prospects. They are just a compendium of questions I assembled in talking to experienced life coaches about what they would ask a newbie life coach if given the chance. However, if you answered no to two or three (or more) of these questions, you might seriously think about putting off the life-coach training.

The qualities of a good life coach are widely known. The qualities of a great life coach are very specific. The characteristics cited by the coaches in this book make a decent place to start. The best advice may be to work like a coach.

LISTENING

PERVIS TAYLOR SAID IT well: "If you can't *listen*, really sit back and pay attention while someone is telling you about their life, then you'll be lost as a life coach." Are you a good listener? Right now, before you make any decisions about life coaching, ask yourself, Can I sit in a conversation and let the other person do all the talking, without interruption, without turning the subject toward my own needs, without resorting to phony reinforcements or empty follow-up questions?

Are you an active listener? Do questions occur to you as you listen? Are you able to form a picture of the people being talked about even if you don't know them? Can you ask (when the time is right) real follow-up questions that expand your understanding?

Go out and practice listening. Eschew the small talk; sit down with someone you meet and ask them a question that requires that they be expansive in their answer. Go to a nursing home and sit with someone who has lived a long time. These people are out there. Or choose a neighbor to whom you haven't paid that much attention up to now. Where did they go last summer? Or where were they during some watershed moment in history? You may have to trade stories to start, but don't let your stories take over the conversation.

MEMORY

As your interlocutor speaks, work to remember every detail you can from their story—the names of other people, the city they were in, what they were doing, who they were working with, and so forth—without writing it down. The key to active listening is a strong ability to remember small details of the speaker's story and connect them to long-term memory cues. Use visualization, mnemonic devices, memory improvement apps. When the other person is finished, can you effortlessly form a question that triggers them to give a second answer in as much or more detail? Test yourself by following up in the days to come.

You don't have to remember names well when you start training as a life coach, but you'd better develop this skill when you start practicing. Or you'd better take good notes after meeting with every client in order not to lose too much time refreshing your memory in your next session with the client.

Asked how she remembered the details of thirty different monthly clients, Markita Collins said: "You have to care! You have to empathize! You need to be able to picture another person's life, their pain and their joy, while they are speaking. Caring is the key. If you can't empathize with the people you're talking about, their words will just float out your head when you stand up to leave. And they will know. They really will."

QUESTIONING

Do you know how to ask questions that get more than the answer you expected when you asked them? Good questions are the bread and butter of good life coaches. Pay attention to what works. What makes the people you know hold forth? What about relative strangers? For the time being, you don't have to sound like a life coach. Just pay attention to what works. Good questions create good rapport. That's what you're aiming for here. Take a few minutes to look up "best life-coaching questions" on the internet. You'll be astounded by what you find. There are scores of pages that can help. Pay attention to the way your questions are constructed. The best questions aren't necessarily "goal-oriented." They often have more than one part. You can also ask for some speculation or wishful thinking, or demand a quick follow-up. At the very least, a question like "What would you do less of if you could change things right now?" should provide you with information that will only do the person in front of you good.

SEEING

CAN YOU MAKE A person feel seen? This is not a matter of remarking on the way they're dressed, or making brief eye contact at the start of a conversation. Acknowledging a person's presence, whether in person or online, is most often a matter of combining the tools just discussed with a sense of respect for the person before you. Amy Moser works to make her students feel seen in the classroom she works in after school in London. "They're young, so sometimes they have trouble even being looked at. Making them feel seen is a first step in registering the importance of what they do. I don't put them on the spot; I try to learn who they are in the work we do together. That's something they remember, that respect. It means a great deal."

READING

WHETHER YOU PLAN TO get certified or not, buy *The Portable Coach: Twenty-Eight Sure-fire Strategies for Business and Personal Success* by life-coach pioneer Thomas Leonard. And read it. Twice. It doesn't matter what sort of coaching you plan to do; this classic in the coaching library gives you a perspective on your potential to make measured changes in your life, linking up to a useful list of individual challenges. It may be a business book at one level, but it's a book about living on every other level. If the questions you've been asked in these pages make no sense when you see them explained in *The Portable Coach*, then life coaching really may not be the field for you.

START FIGURING

DETERMINE YOUR NICHE. ASSESS yourself. List your work experience. Write down your passions. Take a look at the list of specialty-coaching opportunities on pages twelve and thirteen, and make a little check mark next to the ones that might apply to you. Other kinds of lists can help too. Wish lists. Who do you want to help? Skills lists. Job lists. Remember the phlebotomist who worked with Markita Collins, the one who sensed that she was a kind of "mother to all" based on numerous experiences she's had as a caregiver that were unknown to the women she worked with in a maternity clinic. She took that oft-stated, rarely expressed passion in her heart and created a business coaching for young moms.

HIRE A LIFE COACH

WHETHER OR NOT YOU'RE like Gregory Diehl, who hates the term "life coach," you should know by now that almost all life coaches retain the services of a life coach before they ever become one themselves, and many continue to retain a life coach even after starting their own practice. Most established coaches recommend nothing less than this before you ever work as a coach. Many coaches will barter with you for their services when you first consult with them.

Your first life coach can teach you many things that you will later make a part of your practice. Pay attention and ask questions about the methods with which they conduct their sessions; learn about the skill of asking good questions, and observe the inferences they draw from your answers. Note whether you feel comfortable at their pace and with the timing and tone of their responses. Ask them to speak at length about the techniques and approaches they are employing. No life coach keeps a secret, except the ones his clients tell him. Life coaching is very much a pass-along craft, and careers are stitched together by studying the many practitioners out there who can influence the up-and-comer.

CERTIFICATION

EVENTUALLY YOU WILL HAVE to decide whether or not to enter into a life-coach training program. Most coaches will tell you it's a matter of age and experience. A retiring financial officer with a background in Asian studies might want to get on with the job of coaching business execs who are in the process of relocating overseas—and skip the training. But think of Farrell Reynolds, who left the offices of a major cable network and ventured into virtual classrooms of Coach U to obtain certification. To his mind, certification is a virtual requirement for anyone thinking of making the transition into the business of coaching. All coaches acknowledge that training, in the form of online classes, learning modules, attending professional meetings, and joining professional societies, is widely available. It is also true that certified coaches are free to change the orientation of their practice as they go along. Markita Collins, a certified NLP practitioner, reports that she no longer uses NLP techniques in her life-coaching practice, though the training has had an undeniable effect on her work in individual sessions.

Keep in mind that training programs differ radically from one another in terms of time, tuition, and demands on the student. There are training courses that require no more than attendance at a three-hour seminar in a Holiday Inn Express conference room out by the interstate. Advanced training like the International Coach Federation's "personal certified coach" program—a continuing education certification for existing life coaches—demands that professionals have five hundred hours of coaching experience and at least twenty-five clients in order to participate. This program includes training in creating coaching agreements, in coaching ethics, in active listening skills, and in accountability. The ICF's rival organization, the International Association of Coaching (IAC), has similar requirements, which include, among other things, the submission of actual recorded coaching sessions that are assessed in terms of ethical standards and active-listening skills. The IAC offers a widely recommended course that includes training in client assessment and session reporting, professional ethics, and the psychological principles of coaching.

Working as an uncertified coach will require you to drum up your own client base using materials that you picked up from the internet, from attendance at group presentations, and from one-on-one work. You will be responsible for developing a practice that assures follow-up with clients, bookkeeping, advertising, and social media presence. It might be helpful to look for opportunities to join an established firm as a junior partner, as Amy Moser did with Children First.

SHARPEN UP YOUR SOCIAL MEDIA SKILLS

BE LIKE PERVIS TAYLOR. He is a disciplined, creative voice on several platforms. He "meets" new clients online numerous times a week. He follows up with everyone, almost immediately. He has branded himself and his practice so that he is recognized as a leader through his work with young men of color, and as a writer and social media presence. Post regularly, and be thorough in your coverage of your events and thoughtful in the way you speak about your clients. Explore all the lanes of social media traffic. Look at the analytics. Pick the one most suited to you as a special focus, but maintain an active profile on as many as you can. If you are building your practice from scratch, it is likely that it will live or die with your mastery of social media and the tools of branding.

FINALLY

Do people ask you for advice?

When we're kids, it's easy for us to know who we can count on to go to for rock-solid advice. As adults, it's far more difficult to identify who will give advice that is untethered from self-interest and greed. If you want to go into this field, you'll need the ability to motivate others in inventive ways without getting in their way. Should you decide to take on the challenge of being a life coach, remember the ability to motivate others does not come easy. Work hard on the quiet bonds of trust that grow between a life coach and his clients. It is good work. Go on . . .

. . . And don't give them any advice.

CONTACT INFORMATION FOR THE LIFE COACHES IN THIS BOOK

Pervis Taylor

PervisTaylor.com
Twitter: pervistaylor
Instagram: pervistaylor

Farrell Reynolds

FarrellReynolds.com

Amy Moser

www.helpingkids.co.uk

Gregory Diehl

www.gregorydiehl.net
Twitter: GregoryVDiehl

Markita D. Collins

Markitadcollins.com
Twitter: markitadcollins
Instagram: markitadcollins

ACKNOWLEDGMENTS

As always, my love to Chris White. The painter Guy Berard was my life coach in college; I'm especially thankful for our talks. Thanks to Rhonesha Byng for her help in getting to coaches. I have had many coaches in recent years. J.D. Grove, Bill Fenlon, Bryan Langdoc, Tamrha Gatti Richardson, Jim Smith, Cathie Malach, Micah Ling, Abby Chew, Wayne Glausser, and Michael "Doc" Shaw. Thank you.

My children, August, Walter, and Fiona, lead me and surprise me. I am forever grateful.

Most of all: love and thanks to Maia Alley, who has reverse coached me in ways I'm still recognizing.

ABOUT THE AUTHOR

Tom Chiarella is Emeritus Professor of English at DePauw University and longtime writer-at-large for *Esquire*, where he profiled celebrities, athletes, and political figures and penned two columns, "Golf" and "Influence." He's currently a contributor to *Golf* and *Chicago* magazines. He has also written for *The New Yorker*, *Golf Digest*, *Outside*, Wired.com, BleacherReport.com, *Elle UK*, *Fashion*, *O: The Oprah Magazine*, and *Runner's World*. He lives his wife, novelist Chris White, and their granddaughter in Bainbridge, Indiana. He's the author of *Foley's Luck*, *Thursday's Game*, *Writing Dialogue* and *Becoming A Real Estate Agent*.